Thomas Aquinas

Also from Sophia Institute Press
by A. G. Sertillanges:

What Jesus Saw from the Cross

A. G. Sertillanges, O.P.

Thomas Aquinas

Scholar, Poet, Mystic, Saint

Translated by Godfrey Anstruther, O.P.

SOPHIA INSTITUTE PRESS
Manchester, New Hampshire

Thomas Aquinas: Scholar, Poet, Mystic, Saint, an English translation of *Saint Thomas d'Aquin* of the series *Grands Coeurs*, was originally published by Burns, Oates, and Washbourne, Ltd., London, in 1957. This 2011 edition by Sophia Institute Press includes minor editorial revisions.

Printed in the United States of America

Cover design by Carolyn McKinney

On the cover: *St. Thomas Aquinas Reading*, by Fra Bartolommeo, Museo di San Marco dell'Angelico, Florence, Italy / The Bridgeman Art Library.

Sophia Institute Press
Box 5284, Manchester, NH 03108
1-800-888-9344
www.SophiaInstitute.com

Nihil obstat: Fr. Henry St. John, M.A., O.P.
Fr. Richard Kehoe, S.J.L., O.P.
Imprimatur: Fr. Bede Jarrett, O.P., *Provincial*
August 28, 1932

Nihil obstat: Edward J. Mahoney, S.Th.D., *Censor Deputatus*
Imprimatur: Joseph Butt, *Vicarius Generalis*
Westmonasterii, October 20, 1932

Library of Congress Cataloging-in-Publication Data

Sertillanges, A. G. (Antonin Gilbert), 1863-1948
[S. Thomas d'Aquin. English]
Thomas Aquinas : scholar, poet, mystic, saint / A. G. Sertillanges ; translated by Godfrey Anstruther.
p. cm.
Originally translated and pub.: London : Burns, Oates & Washbourne, ltd., 1933.
Includes bibliographical references.
ISBN 978-1-933184-70-8 (pbk. : alk. paper) 1. Thomas, Aquinas, Saint, 1225?-1274 I. Title. II. Title: Saint Thomas Aquinas.
BX4700.T6S4213 2011
230'.2092 — dc22
[B]

2009039541

SPA POD 2025

Contents

Translator's Note

This book appeared in French as one of the series of *Grands Coeurs*, under the simple title *Saint Thomas d'Aquin*. Since it is here published as an isolated work, I have given it a more distinctive title.

As a literal translation would have proved intolerable to English readers, I have at times exercised considerable freedom in translating, without, I hope, any detriment to the author's meaning.

A few minor corrections have been made, with the author's approval.

G. A.

Introduction

All great men have understood their own age and furnished what it sought. This alone marks them out as heroes worthy of our admiration. But if there are among them men who represent our common nature in one of its permanent functions, their work outlives them, and their message makes a fresh appeal to each generation.

St. Thomas is of this number. He had the divine spark. His doctrine contains something whereby it can renew itself from age to age, while his personality, perfect type as he is of scholar, social benefactor, and saint, is a constant example.

It is gratifying to view this double solution of the problem of existence: by abstract thought in his inspired *Summa*, and by example in his heroic life. This one man satisfies the two great ideals that we seek with almost equal zest: the ideal of intelligence and the ideal of holiness. Moreover, so closely are they united in him that he has created a new harmony. Holiness in him is a search for knowledge, and his knowledge is his message.

Today, when the world is in a state of upheaval, blinded by uncontrolled lights, and befogged by undisciplined instincts, today is the moment to bring forth such an example. To lead men to meditate on a mind attuned to all knowledge, a soul given up to the supreme values, is the aim of this little book.

Rosemont
September 8, 1930

Thomas Aquinas

Editor's note: The biblical quotations in the following pages are taken from the Douay-Rheims edition of the Old and New Testaments. Where applicable, quotations have been cross-referenced with the differing names and enumeration in the Revised Standard Version, using the following symbol: (RSV =).

Chapter One

St. Thomas's Epoch

The beginning of the thirteenth century has often been described as a time when revolutionary forces, coupled with confusion of mind, were on the verge of misguiding Christian thought and Christian civilization. Père Mandonnet, O.P., in his classic *Siger de Brabant*, has drawn a vivid picture of that epoch, but it is enough for our present purpose to point out its salient characteristics, as these are sufficiently striking not to need further amplification.

The West was Christian to the core. Christianity had been present when its civilization was formed, had watched over its infancy, inspired its institutions, and nourished its thought with doctrines derived from the Gospel by centuries of development. It thus possessed the greatest possible treasure, a doctrine of life, in those days which our modern topsy-turvy civilization likes to refer to as the "Dark Ages."

Then a crisis arose, comparable to that of the sixteenth century, and due to similar causes. It was a question, then as always, of growth; and the growth of institutions, like the growth of a child, is beset with dangers. If it goes wrong, we call it a decline, and in a society fundamentally sound but still unstable, and only imperfectly adapted to the general laws of human thought and experience, such a decline might well prove fatal.

Like the crisis at the Renaissance, this, too, was a return to antiquity. Greek thought and Greek ideas invaded the Christian West, by the introduction of Arab, Jewish, and Alexandrine philosophy. It was a breath of life, but it came as a cyclone; it was at once a medicine and a poison.

Aristotle became the new God. His writings, inflated by misleading commentaries, were inadequate in themselves, while their excessive naturalism, together with some particularly serious blemishes, threatened to lead Christian thought astray. And they had ardent followers in the schools, who were ready to push them to extremes.

Even the teaching on God was endangered, for Aristotle's treatment of God in the twelfth book of the *Metaphysics* is misleading, despite its highly intellectual character. With great caution it can be explained in a Christian sense, as has indeed been done by St. Thomas, but even then, it is meager and wholly inadequate. God has no definite personality; there is no affirmation of providence, nor even of his freedom in creating. While he is admitted as the final cause, his efficient causality, if not openly denied, is at least made very doubtful.

Similarly, Aristotle makes the soul something above matter; it is "separate"; it comes to the body "from without," as it were "by the door." There is no certitude that it belongs to the individual, that it guarantees him a really spiritual and immortal life, that it makes him really responsible. He leaves it an open question whether morality is a mere whim, or corresponds to a divine order. Everything is vague and ambiguous enough to enable commentators, especially the Arabs, to interpret it in a sinister sense.

People began to be known as Aristotelians, followers of Averroes, Avicenna, Avicebron, and Maimonides, and their Christianity was at a low ebb. Under the aegis of "the Philosopher"[1] and his followers, they disputed the most fundamental and certain of Catholic dogmas. The creation of the world in time, the divine government and Fatherhood, the individuality and immortality of the soul, free will, and moral responsibility gave place to an eternal world, an abstract God cut off from all communication with his creatures, a unique *Intellect* for all men, which alone was immortal, a strict determinism, physical and psychological, which ruled out all responsible action. That was knowledge. The Christian faith, the basis of civilization and the mother of all learning, could not be openly attacked, but there was always this bias, which was later to call forth St. Thomas's most indignant protests.

"We have no doubt," they would say, "that faith is true, but we are speaking as philosophers. As philosophers, we must say *this*; as Christians we may say *that:* a different point of view requires different conclusions; a different learning requires different principles." They began to distinguish, as Jules Soury has done just as seriously, between "Oratory and Laboratory."

Here were two contrary dangers to Christianity: the danger of ignoring the new learning, and the danger of apostasy. To reject the newly found wisdom was to make human reason apparently to contradict itself, while to give way to these forces of paganism and intellectual pride was to open the door to the most pernicious errors, and so risk disaster.

There was only one thing to be done: to take over the new doctrines and restate them: to refine the gold. Instead of casting aside the finest of all human philosophies, out of a kind of cowardly prudence, was it not better for Catholics to adapt it to Christian

[1] Aristotle.

thought, by interpreting, revising, completing it, and thereby to make it their own? That was what St. Thomas set out to do.

But this way out of the difficulty, obvious in retrospect, was not then evident. It is almost the same thing to conceive a plan, and to be able to carry it out. It was so much easier to make protests, to react violently, and to go to the other extreme.

There was an influential school of mysticism, going back to St. Augustine and St. Bernard, steeped for the greater part in Franciscan spirituality, which opposed the Aristotelian and rationalistic movement. This school willingly went to the lengths of exalting faith to the detriment of reason and knowledge, whose very autonomy, methods, and principles were viewed with suspicion. Aristotle was suspect, and so also were those who tried to introduce his dialectics and his views into theology. Its horror at the excesses of the extremists was natural, but it was hostile to the very Renaissance as well, on the grounds that it menaced the ancient Faith.

What was the use of research and subtle argument when one could obtain certitude from the fountainhead? This pride of intellect could only unsettle people, bring up a lot of useless questions, and prepare the way for heresy and schism. There were plenty of names that could be cited in evidence of the danger due to these novelties; arrogant thinkers, who threw aside all authority, went so far with their rationalism as to seem to have lost all shreds of Christianity, and who claimed to prove and control everything, even God's word.

So far had things gone that the relation between faith and reason was by now an insoluble question. St. Anselm and others had found it a stumbling-block. Peacemaker, mystic, philosopher though he was, equally at home in dialectics and in contemplation, Anselm could not settle the problem satisfactorily. Rational mysticism and theological rationalism fought it out in the dark.

They could not trace the passage from what was demonstrated to what was believed, from science to dogma, and were led to a total disregard for the one, which meant the virtual destruction of the other. They lost themselves in a maze of questions, in their attempt to clear them up; they clouded with doubt the very theses they prided themselves on proving; or, on the other hand, they rejected every kind of demonstration, even where it was admissible. Was there any way out?

Ecclesiastical authorities, appealed to by both sides, hesitated between stemming the tide of progress, and countenancing the scandalous abuses of Paris and of its Faculty of Arts, which threatened to corrupt the whole of Christianity. They compromised by indecisive measures. They condemned nothing absolutely, except the errors that were self-condemned, but they issued provisional prohibitions to check the evil, in the vain hope of better times, which seemed never to come.

There is nothing extraordinary about this perplexity. Human reason has ever been a source of danger to religious minds. Its very grandeur as the image of God, and its apparent close intimacy with us, renders it domineering, deceptive, and self-sufficient.

The Middle Ages were credulous, but they were young, and full of vigor and originality, just as prone to the sublime as to the ridiculous, unbalanced, and curious to a degree of presumption. They were used to the warm climate of faith, and were suddenly plunged into the cold air of philosophy. Would they have the stamina to resist the change? A badly managed crisis would leave them permanent invalids. They had to be saved without drastic measures, and the only thing to do was to resort to temporary alleviation, and wait for a better time.

They had to find out whether this Aristotle, taken as a whole, with due allowance made for his obvious lapses, was friend or foe.

Could they work with him? Was he a treacherous ally or an insidious enemy? If only he had been alone! But, alas, he had a following of Jews and Arabs who gave him an artificial glory and obscured his real greatness. The Pope made up his mind that, at all costs, the faithful must be protected. Aristotle was twice forbidden to be taught in the schools as an "author." This did not anathematize him, and there was nothing to prevent his being read as a classic in private. Moreover, the ban was only temporary — "until he shall have been revised." But who was to revise him?

At the moment when St. Thomas's intellectual life began, the question was not absolutely decided. Albert the Great had undertaken "to render the works of Aristotle intelligible to the Latins," and to assimilate their substance. He worked with energy but he was not sufficiently orderly or methodical. He touched on questions without fully settling them; his expositions were confused; his textual equipment was incomplete, being taken from translations that were inaccurate and full of glosses. His knowledge was encyclopedic. His genius was rather to collect materials than to synthesize. In a word, despite his truly great personal fame, he was not the man to direct his age and lead the Church to safety.

Abelard, a few decades before, had prepared the way. He was a dialectician of repute, fully aware of the need of providing the Faith with rational weapons, by the introduction of philosophy. He became the pioneer of the new reform, but did it more harm than good in the long run. Although he had no lack of courage, he was not sure of his ground. His outbursts, exaggerated, it is true, by overzealous mystics, gave a bad name to his propositions and methods, while his better work was spoiled by its sketchiness. The real leader was yet to come.

St. Thomas's Epoch

The human race is ever restless; it goes through a cycle of phases. Ideas are conceived, brought forth, developed; then comes a crisis, and the cycle begins over again. In the history of Christianity, there are outstanding epochs when new forces providentially appear. By reason of their antecedent phases, whose import is only now recognized, they seem to extend far into the past, even as they exert an influence over the future. The progress of the gospel is an excellent example.

In the third and fourth centuries, the Fathers made a great effort to harmonize Christian doctrine with what remained of ancient thought, then on the decline — a real attempt to rediscover this thought, make it their own, and weld it into a complete synthesis. This is brought out by M. Aimé Puech in his fine *Histoire de la littérature grecque chrétienne*.

But those days were long past, and a turbulent period succeeded them. Intellectual life dwindled almost to nothing, and then revived. A long period of gestation and sporadic achievements ended with the century of St. Louis, and a renaissance was imminent. In this hour of greatness and hope, Aristotle, the Philosopher *par excellence*, returned. He was a dangerous tool and difficult to use. It was not enough that the work should be waiting to be done. "There must be some chance, something unforeseen," says Nietzsche, "in order that a great man, in whom lies dormant the solution of a problem, may set to work at the appointed time: in order that he may, as it were, shine out."

St. Thomas was providentially raised to fill this role, and he succeeded in spite of all opposition. Let us say something of his formation.

Chapter Two

St. Thomas's Life

Emerson has observed that "great geniuses have the shortest biographies."[2] This is particularly true of the great thinkers. It is much easier to recount facts than thoughts, and a thinker must be understood before he can be described.

When, however, the thought has been really lived, and an effective philosophy has resulted, why not look to it for supplementary data?

St. Thomas belonged to a noble family, related through his father, Landulf, to Frederick Barbarossa, and through his mother, Theodora of Teano, to the Norman barons. Landulf was a rugged man, and somewhat violent, as was to be expected in that age of wars. The countess Theodora was an energetic, ambitious woman with a will of her own. St. Thomas's elder brothers, Landulf and Raynald, were both in Frederick II's army.

St. Thomas, the youngest son, was born about 1225, probably at the beginning of that year. He was born in the family castle of Roccaseca near Naples. Caustic opponents were ready to point

[2] Ralph Waldo Emerson, *Representative Men*, "Plato."

out the symbolic meaning of this. The *Summa Theologica* was a rock as "dry" as that of the Counts of Aquin. However . . .

The famous abbey of Monte Casino was not far from the castle, and it was there that St. Thomas, at the age of five or six, was sent to study, under his uncle Abbot Sinibald. He was a fine-looking boy; mothers would watch him as he passed their doors, and he was loved by the poor, whom he assisted with whatever he could get from his home. When the servants complained of this, his delighted mother would tell them to let him continue his alms-giving. It is told of him that one day, when he was quite a baby and was about to be bathed, his nurse tried to take from his hand a piece of parchment that he would not surrender. On it was found the *Ave Maria*.

It is not absolutely certain, but highly probable that when he went to Monte Casino, he went, not as a noble pupil, but as a little monk, an *oblate*, and that he wore the Benedictine habit. His parents hoped that one day he would take over the vast revenues of the abbey and would use his influence on behalf of his own household. Religion and worldly interest were very much confused in those days. The abbey controlled seven bishoprics, supported armies, and was strongly fortified. In 1229, it had been besieged and taken by Frederick II in person, aided by the Count of Aquin, and when peace was restored, the sending of St. Thomas there was doubtless a kind of pledge, like a marriage made to ratify an alliance.

St. Thomas showed a marked taste for study and quiet, and a surprising lack of interest in noise and games. He was ever anxiously inquiring, "What is God?" and his whole life was to be an attempt to answer that question. The abbey, with its culture and learning, had a broadening influence on his mind; he learned to appreciate the beauty of the liturgy and of knowledge and took a larger and grander view of the world about him.

New conflicts between the Pope and the emperor caused the monks to be dispersed, and St. Thomas returned home. The abbot had discovered his extraordinary bent for study, and, doubtless desirous of gaining an illustrious subject later on, advised that he should be sent to the University of Naples to do what we should now call his humanities. He was then about fourteen years old. Little is known about his life there beyond the fact that he soon won fame for his learning and was far ahead of his class.

In 1244, at the age of about nineteen, his life took a different turn. For some twenty years, a learned, active order had been meeting with remarkable success. The Friars Preachers were university men, and they recruited most of their members from among the university professors and students. They devoted their lives to study, preaching, and learning. In Paris, in a single term, seventy-two students and professors had joined their ranks. It was like the astonishing growth of the early Church over again, and naturally proved a great attraction to a young man like St. Thomas.

The "modern" order had a monastic life as flourishing as that of Monte Casino, and a much more vigorous intellectual life. St. Thomas had nothing to lose and much to gain by joining it. He changed the black habit for the black and white: he relinquished the purely contemplative life for one that implied an equal sacrifice and a greater service. For the motto of the new order was *Contemplata aliis tradere*,[3] which has an especial appeal to one seeking perfection.

Nor did he consider this move as showing any lack of filial piety; he was free. He was not tied to the Benedictine Order by the provisional *vow* of his parents, and he was not interested in his

[3] "To pass on to others the fruits of contemplation."

family's ambitions. Young men, and especially young men of his caliber, are too generous to be influenced by such considerations. His father had died the year before, 1243, so that there was no fear of opposition from the head of the family, but he had still to face his mother and his two brothers.

As a matter of fact, he had only just received the habit from Thomas d'Agni, the Prior of San Domenico Maggiore, when the countess Theodora arrived to reclaim her son. She was told that he had left for Rome. She hurried thither, only to find that he had set out for Paris, where he had been sent by his superiors to complete his studies. Exasperated and determined to show that she was mistress of her own family, she sent to her sons in Frederick's army to use every means to cut off St. Thomas's escape.

Meanwhile, in company with the Master-General, John the Teutonic, and three other friars, St. Thomas was making for Bologna. They had stopped to rest by a fountain when the saint's brothers suddenly appeared. Without waiting to argue, they tried to tear his habit from him, but he resisted them. Being loath to do him violence, they forced him onto a horse and led him off to imprison him in the castle of St. John, not far from Roccaseca.

Here he was confined and allowed neither to go out nor to see any other Dominican. They tried to subdue him by hardships, but that simply enabled him to practice strictly the rule of his order, from which they were trying to win him, while he made the solitude his novitiate and went on with his studies unperturbed. His fellow-religious found some means of communicating with him and sent him books: the Bible, the *Sophisms* of Aristotle, and the *Sentences* of Peter Lombard.

His sisters, Theodora and Marietta, were ordered to use their persuasion with him. He received them kindly, but their visits had just the opposite effect. One sister became a Benedictine nun, and abbess of the convent at Capua, so well did she learn that the greatest manifestation of sisterly affection was to help her brother to desert her.

Then they tried another kind of persecution. His brothers, home from the army, tried a method more in keeping with their own way of life. They brought a friend of theirs from Naples, a beautiful woman, and let her into the tower.

The present Pope once made the striking remark, that "if St. Thomas's purity had failed at this critical moment, it was very likely that the Church would never have had an Angelic Doctor,"[4] which goes to show how great is our responsibility when such a boon to the whole Church can depend on a private struggle.

St. Thomas did not succumb. Without a word, he drove the woman from the room with a brand, and burned a cross on the wall as a sign of his victory. The following night, his biographers relate, while he slept, he was visited by two angels who girded him with a cord of fire, and he awoke with a cry. That was the end of all temptation against purity. His confessor and friend, Reginald, was able to state to William of Tocco, one of the witnesses for his canonization, that his general confession on his deathbed was, in this matter, like the confession of a child of five.

After that, he seems to have been less carefully guarded. With the connivance of his sisters, and possibly even of his mother, certainly with the help of the monks, he contrived to escape and was let down from his tower "by means of a rope." Later, the legend grew that he was let down in a basket like St. Paul. His family offered no further opposition, and seemed even to consent, "overcome by his constancy." The confinement had lasted a year and some months.

[4] Pope Pius XI, "On St. Thomas Aquinas."

Nothing had been lost by this delay; he was only the more confirmed in his vocation, which he now pursued from the point at which it had been interrupted. He set out for Paris with John the Teutonic, to study under Albert the Great, the most learned man of his times, and the one who, as we have seen, prepared the materials for that synthesis of doctrine which was to be St. Thomas's life-work. The workman was sent to him; he fashioned him, foretold his future greatness, and might have said with St. John the Baptist: "He must increase, but I must decrease."[5] But they remained associated in the work, and their names are inseparable.

Fortunate it was that such a genius should receive his formation by six years of intimate association with a master like Albert the Great. He was an intrepid worker, a first-class intelligence, generous, a brother-religious, and a father — a splendid influence for the young, ardent, omnivorous mind of St. Thomas.

St. Thomas appeared so quiet that at Cologne he was nicknamed the great "dumb ox," but he was living a life of intense activity. He was twenty years old and fully grown. In spite of his broad shoulders, he was delicate and extremely sensitive. "The least bodily ill upset him." Delicacy of body is, according to Aristotle, a sign of an acute intelligence. At present, his charm was his youth, with his generous, simple personality, as pure and limpid as a diamond.

St. Thomas's arrival at Paris in 1245 coincided with the fair reign of St. Louis; it was then that the *Sainte-Chapelle* was built.

[5] John 3:30.

The University of Paris was in its heyday; it was the home of study, although a somewhat riotous one, and the entire intellectual world met there. Paris was, in the words of Albert the Great, "the city of Philosophers." But St. Thomas did not stay here long. The Dominican *Studium* of Saint-Jacques was soon overcrowded, and the order had just opened a *Studium Generale* at Cologne, where Albert was sent as Regent of Studies. St. Thomas went with him. It was a matter of obedience, although it is hardly likely that he found it a wrench to leave Paris, as he was indifferent to his surroundings, his home being in the domain of knowledge.

At Cologne he devoted his time more and more to learning and solitude. He led the hidden life. We might apply to him what Carlyle says of Cromwell before he began his campaigns: "He had *lived* silent; a great unnamed sea of Thought round him all his days."[6]

His silence led his companions to imagine that he had a touch of brain-fog. One of them offered to help him, and he humbly accepted the offer. All went well until, one day, the instructor got into difficulties and St. Thomas charitably helped him out, thereby showing his natural bent to teach.

However, an incident was soon to arouse the dumb ox from his silence. His biographers recount it with much relish, and no doubt embroider it, although it represents substantially his sudden urge of self-expression, like a child's first attempt to talk. What was then spontaneous and almost unconscious became afterward a recognized duty.

This is the story. Albert was giving a course of lectures on the *Divine Names* of Dionysius. Thomas took down some notes, a page of which fell, by chance, into the hands of Saint Albert. He was

[6] Thomas Carlyle, *Heroes and Hero-Worship*, lect. 6.

utterly astonished and decided to probe his knowledge and, if possible, to unveil it and put an end to all doubts. He therefore invited St. Thomas to get ready for a public debate, and, when the day came, he himself stood as his opponent. Albert put forward four subtle objections, and everyone thought that St. Thomas was worsted. But no: he put an end to the debate with a masterly distinction. "You do not speak," said Albert, "as one on the defensive, but as a master expounding the truth." St. Thomas modestly answered, "I can see no other way of replying to the objections." He already realized that a clear, positive exposition of the truth will answer all objections and put an end to quibbling.

It was then that Albert prophesied, "You call him a dumb ox, but the time will come when so loud will be the bellowing of his doctrine, that it will resound to the ends of the earth." Rather solemn words, and hardly those of a master to his pupil, but we do not vouch for their historical accuracy.

At all events, St. Thomas was henceforth made to give a course himself, and the manuscript of his treatise on the *Divine Names*, in his own rapid, difficult handwriting, is still extant as a part of his course on *Ethics*.

It was at this time, about 1250, that St. Thomas had an opportunity of finally settling his vocation. His family fell upon bad times. His brother Raynald was put to death by the emperor for siding with the Holy See, and the castle of Aquin was sacked. At the death of the emperor, a little later, Theodora appealed to St. Thomas to save the family from ruin. His vocation was no obstacle, as the Pope had granted him a dispensation to become Abbot of Monte Casino, without giving up his Dominican habit. It seemed his duty to accept this compromise, but he knew better and refused.

Later on, a further attempt was made. He was offered the Archbishopric of Naples, with the revenues of the rich abbey of Saint Pierre. The prospects were brilliant: he would be archbishop at an unusually early age; he was wonderfully gifted and well connected. What more could he want?

But he had other ambitions. He was to serve the world, not by ruling in a brilliant court, but by his knowledge. He had his allotted task, and he made up his mind. He must carry on the work that Albert had begun. In God's providence he was to be knight, Benedictine, Dominican, persecuted and tried, student, and then, Doctor and saint. These successive phases sum up his whole life.

The time had come to begin in earnest. Albert proposed Thomas as a bachelor for Paris, the first step to the degree of Master. This needed the approbation of the Master-General, and John the Teutonic, although a friend of St. Thomas and one who knew his worth, refused. The proper age for a bachelor at Paris was thirty-five, not twenty-seven. But there was at Cologne another Dominican, Cardinal Hugo of St. Cher, and Albert found in him a powerful ally. He pointed out the necessity of sending to Paris a pupil so promising, and of using his great gifts to further the work that Albert himself had begun.

The Master-General gave way before their combined pressure; St. Thomas returned to Paris as bachelor and began teaching immediately (1252). He made a brilliant start and, in four years, had established his reputation and laid the foundations of his first writings. He commentated, orally and in writing, on the four Books of the Sentences, the then-classic manual of theology, and brought out his first philosophical treatise, *De Ente et Essentia.*[7]

[7] "On Being and Essence."

It is worth noting that in his very first course, a trace of which we find in his Commentary on the *Sentences*,[8] he sketched his method and, as it were, gave a synopsis of his whole intellectual position.

In 1256, by a papal dispensation, he was admitted to the Licentiate, four years before the statuted age. He began his new work at the same time as St. Bonaventure, who, although his opponent in matters doctrinal, was a greatly valued friend of his. He now had the right to teach unsupervised, and his course opened with a solemn inaugural address known as the *Principium*.

His biographers tell us that this first lecture was dictated to him in a dream, when he was diffident about himself, and could not think what to say. He felt the weight of responsibility in occupying a professional chair and addressing an audience, to say nothing of the greater, unseen audience of readers.

The strife was about to begin. It seems a strong word to use, but it has historical support. Despite St. Thomas's objectivity in thought and expression, he was an ardent, passionate personality and a redoubtable antagonist.

The first quarrel was when William of St. Amour launched a campaign against the religious orders. The dispute, which had been going on for some time, now centered on St. Thomas, as he occupied a chair of theology, which the secular clergy wished to suppress, particularly when they saw with envy the success with which his teaching was met.

It was high time that somebody brought the matter to a head, for Pope Innocent IV, disquieted by the patent abuses in the

[8] Q. 1, art. 1.

religious orders, had issued bull after bull against them. He felt that the Church had lost its equilibrium and that there was danger to the hierarchy from the sudden growth and invasion of the mendicant orders, which seemed to exercise an undue influence over the whole Church.

Innocent died three months after the promulgation of his last bull, and his successor, Alexander IV, finding most of his fears unfounded, was content with demanding certain sacrifices from the orders, in return for their full rights. St. Thomas was charged with the defense of the Dominicans.

He was summoned to Anagni, where he published his treatise *Contra impugnantes Dei cultum*,[9] and that soon restored peace. By the Pope's orders, he was made Master, and returned to Paris triumphant, to continue his life of intense teaching and writing.

From 1256 until 1259, he presided at public disputations on *Truth* and kindred questions, and published the treatise *De Veritate*, one of his greatest works. His commentaries on Saint Matthew and on the *De Trinitate* of Boëthius were both written about this time. His reputation grew by leaps and bounds. He was admired, says a contemporary of his, for his brevity, clarity, easy style, and obliging disposition.

But what most impressed people (although some today may think it strange) was the novelty of his teaching. William of Tocco stresses this in the following significant passage: "He brought up new questions, inaugurated a new and valuable method of research and demonstration, and developed new arguments. Those who heard him resolving difficulties and problems in a new way, with new principles, believed that he had been endowed by God with a new light of understanding."

[9] "Against the Adversaries of the Religious State."

In 1259, we find him at Valenciennes, where, with Albert the Great and Peter of Tarantaise, he reorganized the studies of the order and decided on new houses of study in Spain. At the wish of St. Raymond of Penafort, and by the express command of Alexander IV, he undertook the *Summa contra Gentiles*, to help in spreading Christian philosophy in Muslim countries.

This work he wrote, however, in Italy, whither he was called in 1261, to assist at the court of Urban IV. He spent ten years at Anagni, Orvieto, Rome, and Viterbo, consolidating his teaching and making it acceptable to high ecclesiastical authorities. He took advantage of the mass of manuscripts of all nationalities, which had found their way to Rome, and formed the nucleus of the Vatican Library. While he was in Paris, he had been fortunate to be able to consult the fine collection of manuscripts that St. Louis had formed near the *Sainte-Chapelle* and which provided the materials for the *Speculum* of his contemporary Vincent of Beauvais. But at Rome it was his genius rather than his erudition that called for admiration. The poet Henry of Würzburg wrote of his stay there, "He could have discovered philosophy anew, if it had been destroyed by fire. He could have restored it in a better way: his knowledge entitled him to fame, greater even than that of the ancients."[10]

During these years, he wrote his commentaries on Job and Isaiah; the commentary on St. Luke's Gospel (now lost); the *Catena Aurea*, a commentary on the Gospels, made up from the writings of the Fathers; and his main theological and philosophical treatises — namely, *De Potentia*, dealing with God's activity, creation and government; *De Malo*, on the nature of moral evil; *Quaestiones de Spiritualibus Creaturis*, *Quaestiones de Anima*, *Quaestiones de Unitate Verbi Incarnati*, and others.

[10]Quoted by Grabmann, *H. Thomas von Aquin*.

To help in healing the Schism of the West, he wrote *Contra Errores Graecorum*. In 1264 he wrote the Office for the Feast of Corpus Christi, having himself been partly responsible for its institution. Lastly, with William of Moerbeke, a Flemish Dominican and a distinguished Greek scholar, he set about explaining the principal works of Aristotle, and the much-used Platonist *Liber de Causis*. He was the first to employ textual exegesis, which is so important a part of all true criticism. He could not possibly have finished all these works while in Italy, and doubtless continued them at Paris.[11]

In 1265, he was put in charge of the *Studium Generale*, which had recently been founded at Rome by Charles of Anjou. He lived at Santa Sabina. In 1267, he was summoned by the Pope to Viterbo, and it was somewhere about this time that he first conceived the idea of his *Summa Theologica*.

He realized that his teaching was at last definitely accepted, and that he would have the sanction of responsible authorities for the vast plan that he had conceived. We shall return to this later on. He was already known as *Doctor Catholicus*, *Doctor Communis*, and by his proposed masterpiece he was destined to make his influence endure throughout the ages.

The purpose of the *Summa* was to coordinate, in a didactic but simple form, free from the obscurities in contemporary writings, the ideas he had elaborated during his years of study and teaching. It was to be a synthetic, illuminating, methodical work, for the use of young students. The *Prima Pars*, the most important doctrinally, was completed in two years.

Toward the end of 1268, St. Thomas was recalled to Paris, where the university was in a state of disorder, intellectual and moral.

[11] These dates are not certain, and authorities do not agree on them.

The persecution of the religious orders was still active, and, under the influence of Siger of Brabant and Boëthius of Dace, Averroism had gained a hold. Averroists maintained that there was only one intellect for all mankind, and they thereby ruled out all individual immortality. They claimed to derive their doctrine from Aristotle, and their excesses did much to prejudice that revival of Aristotle which St. Thomas had set his heart on. St. Thomas entered the lists, and took the side of Aristotle against the Averroists.

The culminating point of the dispute was his treatise *De Unitate Intellectus contra Averroistas*, written according to Mandonnet in 1270. The reader may judge how bitter the quarrel had become by the concluding paragraph of his work, so unlike the saint's usual calm manner:

> If anyone, boasting of knowledge falsely so called, wishes to say anything against what I have written, let him not speak in corners or to children, who are no judges of such difficult matters, but let him write against this treatise, if he dare: and he will find not only me, who am the least of all, but many others, lovers of truth, who will confound his error, or put an end to his ignorance.

After various fluctuations of fortune, St. Thomas was acclaimed victor, and medieval art records his victory. A picture by Benozzo Gozzoli, in the Louvre, represents Averroes crushed under the foot of the Doctor in glory. Antonello da Messina, in the Palazzo Bellomo at Syracuse, makes his plight even more lamentable: he lies flat on his back, pointing a finger at his vanquisher. Fra Angelico at St. Mark's, and Andrea de Bonaiuto at Santa Maria Novella, with greater kindness depict him sitting at the feet of St. Thomas, deep in thought, and, as it were, preparing for his conversion. All these are graphic commentaries on the last words of the *Opusculum*.

At the same time, St. Thomas had to defend himself against certain followers of St. Augustine, who attacked a number of his tenets, particularly the unity of the vital principle in man, and the philosophical possibility of an eternal world. He published a tract on the latter question entitled *De Æternitate Mundi contra Murmurantes*. The murmuring did not trouble him greatly. In the course of the tract, he let drop a rather caustic remark, the only one (if we except the quotation from *De Unitate Intellectus)* to be found in all his works: "Those who see contradictions here have, doubtless, more subtle intellects than ours: they only are truly men and wise."

In this quarrel, however, he was running the risk of evoking ecclesiastical censure. The Bishop of Paris Stephen Tempier, a former chancellor of the university, was personally very hostile to Aristotle, and hardly friendly to the religious orders. He viewed the progress of Averroism with just alarm and held solemn sessions, where St. Thomas was invited to explain his teaching and where he was vehemently attacked from all sides. His opponents tried to expose him as disloyal to authority, overzealous for the privileges granted to the orders, and abused by them. They tried in particular to show that his Aristotelianism had led him to favor the Averroists, and to run counter to the Faith.

St. Thomas, unruffled, had a clear answer to each of these charges, reassured the authorities of his orthodoxy, without relinquishing any of his principles, and was thus able to save his own propositions from the censure that fell on thirteen others. We shall see, however, that this was only a lull in the storm.

Despite these disturbances, which so agitated the university as to cause a split and, in 1272, a veritable strike, St. Thomas went on writing. It was at this time that he completed the *Secunda Pars* of the *Summa*, a masterpiece of moral theology, which even his most virulent opponents could not but admire. He also continued his commentaries on Aristotle, namely, on the *Perihermenias*, *Metaphysics*, *De Coelo et Mundo*, *De Meteorologica*, *De Generatione*, and began the commentary on the *Politics*. He wrote concurrently, *De Regimine Judaeorum*, *De Occultis Operationibus Naturae*, *De Mixtione Elementorum*, *De Judiciis Astrorum*, *De Sortibus*, *De Motu Gordis*, etc. To these must be added *De Substantiis Separatis*, written certainly later than 1268, and his commentary on St. John's Gospel.

In 1272, St. Thomas left Paris. His colleagues there were so upset at his removal that they appealed to the General Chapter of the Order held at Florence. He was ordered to found a new *Studium Generale* in Italy, at some town of his own choosing. Thomas, doubtless at the request of Charles of Anjou, chose Naples. It was like returning home, but his stay was short-lived. He was played out; his strength had been undermined by continual work. Still, he went on with the *Summa*, the third part of which he had hardly begun at Paris. He got as far as the questions on Penance, and then he felt his courage failing him. An incident affecting his inner life, which we shall return to, made him all the less anxious to continue his work. He hung his harp on the willows by the river, says an old biographer, because he had caught a glimpse of heaven.

In 1274, he was summoned by Gregory X to the General Council of Lyons. He was taken ill on the way and put up at the Castle of Maienza, where his niece lived. He grew worse and asked to be removed to the Cistercian Abbey of Fossa-Nuova, so that he might die in a religious house. When he reached the monastery, he touched the wall and exclaimed, "This is my rest forever and ever."[12] He who had received his earliest training under

[12] Ps. 131:14 (RSV = Ps. 132:14).

the influence of St. Benedict, returned to him to die, and the two great orders were drawn together still closer by the bonds of friendship.

The monks received him with veneration, happy in the thought that he had entrusted his frail body to their keeping. He suffered from the cold, and they insisted on personally cutting and carting the wood for his fire, remarking that it was an honor too great to be given to beasts of burden. "Why," asked the saint, "do these holy men wish to serve me like this? I am only a mere mortal."

He lingered for a month, and in acknowledgment of the monks' hospitality, dictated at their request a short commentary on the *Canticle of Canticles*. He asked for the Last Sacraments, and before his Communion, he exclaimed, "I receive Thee, price of my redemption, food of my journey, for whose love I have studied, kept vigil, and spent myself. Never have I knowingly opposed Thee in anything, but if I should have done so through ignorance, I willingly retract it. I leave everything to the correction of the Church, in obedience to whom I leave this world."

He was about forty-nine years old. Thought, like a raging fire, had used up his strength. But longevity is not essential to genius and does not greatly affect its output. Genius is gauged by its height and its depth. It is its extent that matters; the multiplication of its fruits adds little to its glory, and not much to its services. Michelangelo lived to be ninety; Raphael died at the age of thirty-seven: but what difference there may be between them is due to quite other causes. St. Thomas had lived long enough to give his message; his prodigious mind had borne its fruit, and he went because his hour had come. And his death was but the harbinger of that worldwide influence which he was to exercise over generations to come.

Thomas Aquinas

The reader might like to know a little more about St. Thomas's personality. In his works, his personality is hidden behind his thought, and his very thought is hidden behind the simple clarity of his language. We may speak freely. Other great men, outside their sphere of greatness, might have a mannerism or something about them that is suspicious, or puerile, or perhaps ridiculous, or even hideous. Not so St. Thomas: his personality is as perfect as his works.

He was corpulent and tall — sufficiently tall to attract the notice of farm-laborers as he passed by. He was brown, "the color of new wheat," with an imposing head, a trifle bald, with a powerful, peaceful face, well-formed lips, penetrating eyes, and a quiet, frank expression. He was extremely sensitive to physical pain, but could endure it by concentrating on a problem, as was his wont when he underwent the "minutio," or blood-letting, or when the ulcers on his legs were most painfully cauterized.

There is a widespread legend that he was afraid of storms. This would not be surprising, but it is not true. Once even, when in real danger at sea, he was the only one who kept his head. He had the pious habit of making the Sign of the Cross when it thundered.

He slept little, and often he would break his rest to consult some work, and especially to dictate. He was painfully bored by meals, being always absorbed and preoccupied in "adapting his thought to the world," which he considered was a philosopher's purpose in life; he neglected that other adaptation on which life depends. As he did not put into practice the principle *primo vivere*, "life first of all," he was given Brother Reginald to look after him, and almost to nurse him.

He was silent even when a boy, and grew more and more so as he become more and more engrossed in his work. Ordinary affairs of the world interested him only insofar as they were related to abstract thought, or when charity demanded it. "No occupation," says William of Tocco, "ever altered the direction of his mind."

He was kind and cordial to all, spoke little, and never without good cause; he mixed as little as possible in crowds. By way of recreation, he would walk alone along the cloisters, at great speed, head erect and uncovered. He went out rarely and only when it was necessary. He made his work an excuse for refusing invitations even to the court of St. Louis, and his only visit there was under obedience.

The story of how he behaved on that occasion is well known. In the middle of dinner, he suddenly struck the table and exclaimed, "Now that settles the Manicheans." The prior who was present was afraid that the king would be offended, but, on the contrary, a scribe was sent for to take down the saint's new argument.

He was detached from what most appealed to the majority of men: what seemed to them vital was to him of no importance. One day, he was returning from Saint-Denis and saw stretched out below the whole city of Paris. Asked if he would not like to possess it, he replied that he would rather have a certain manuscript of St. John Chrysostom which he lacked.

He does not seem to have been greatly interested in the spectacle of nature; he lived in its causes and reconstructed them in himself: the soul is "potentially all things." He was interested in men, only as so many souls, and not at all in the bustle and business of the world. Except where some doctrine is at stake, we find hardly any trace of history in his works.

He was simple and uneccentric, and he seems to have been as tranquil as his literary style. It is remarkable that so unsensational a writer should gain a worldwide public.

He was endowed with great intellectual, as well as physical, sensitiveness, but he dominated it and subdued it. If in his writings he appears scarcely human, it is because of his stern mental discipline, and not from any lack of human feelings.

This gave him extraordinary self-control in his controversies. The liturgy hails him as "Pugilist of the Faith"; his life was one of incessant fighting: yet he is "very patient" and "very prudent." We never find him disconcerted by a reverse, or irritated by a contradiction, even of those principles which he held most dear. One of his most intrepid opponents, John Peckham, writing long afterward of an interview in which he had attacked the saint with extreme vehemence, was forced to admit that St. Thomas had replied "with rare gentleness and humility."

In a word, his writings are eminently impersonal, in the good sense of the word, precisely because he was disinterested, kind, open to conviction, impartial, and balanced. Impersonality is as much a mark of his character as of his works. Wisdom was his only passion, and we can discover in his works, despite their sternly impersonal character, a yearning to serve others for the highest motives, hoping for nothing thereby.

His contemporaries speak of him as "wonderfully kind," *miro modo benignus*. He was ready to help others, not only with his mind, but with his body as well. A lay-brother one day, not knowing who he was, took him on an errand around the town, and hurried him on. St. Thomas struggled along as best he could, without a word, and when bystanders protested at the lay-brother's impudence, he only smiled.

He had a ready trust in everybody and would never think ill of another without definite evidence. One day, by way of a joke, a young fellow-religious said to him suddenly, "Brother Thomas, look at this ox flying!" St. Thomas walked quietly to the window, and, when they burst out laughing, he remarked, "I should be less surprised to see an ox flying, than to find a religious lying." Said, no doubt, with his tongue in his cheek, but an indication of his character all the same.

The witnesses for his canonization extol the kind way he received people, the urbanity of his manner, his thorough good nature, his generosity, patience, prudence, piety, and the reasonableness of his charity, giving convincing instances of each.

His grace of manner and charming simplicity were, perhaps, his best-known and most-loved traits, although not the most important. We cannot help contrasting these homely characteristics with all that he stands for, as Doctor, in the eyes of the world. The hero of the pictures of his *Triumph*, the subject of panegyrics, can, without loss of dignity, joke about his *embonpoint*, and his proverbial absentmindedness. When he obtained, through the intercession of St. Agnes, the cure of his beloved Reginald of Piperno, who had a malignant fever, St. Thomas promised to provide the students of the convent at Naples with an annual dinner, on the feast of St. Agnes. He thenceforth charged the King of Naples one ounce of gold per month for his lectures. He was able, alas, to keep his promise only once, as he was approaching his end; but that does not make the incident any the less delightful.

He formed deep friendships, above all with his loyal and constant companion, Reginald, and with his master St. Albert. After St. Thomas's death, Albert could not speak of him without tears, and when far advanced in years, he undertook the journey from Cologne to Paris, which in those days was hardly a comfortable one, in order to defend the memory and the doctrine of his pupil.

Thomas Aquinas

The childlike simplicity of his private life, and the solid, balanced, calm character of his public teaching are the salient features of St. Thomas. Yet he seems today hardly a human being, hardly real, so obscured is his private character by the impersonal character of his thought.

Chapter Three

The Task of St. Thomas

"Great men," says Emilio Castelar, "are different embodiments of great ideas." So, before we go on to speak of St. Thomas's method and success, we must first find out from history what great idea he embodied and how he envisaged his task.

It should be obvious from what has gone before. We have seen him set on solving the problems of his times; we know what those problems were. Granted that he was in truth a great man, the rest should follow. But we can be a little more explicit. There are complications, certainly, but his task is quite simple in its general aim, for the very reason that M. Bergson is thinking of when he says, "All fruitful philosophical work is the outcome of mental concentration, with a pure emotion at its base." What is the primary emotion to which St. Thomas's work corresponds? What did he foresee? Toward what did he, instinctively or intentionally, direct his whole life?

There can be no doubt that his goal was the establishment of the mutual relations of faith and reason, by harmonizing an already existing philosophical system with the apparently disparate notions contained in tradition and contemporary thought. This he realized from the first, owing to his training under Albert the Great, and still more to his own vigorous reaction, which teaching may lead to, but cannot take the place of.

This, his principal aim, is the key to his whole life's work: his message, as we now call it. And his message is of value, if reason and faith make up the whole man; if Aristotle's doctrine can be termed, whether we agree with it or not, "the natural metaphysics of the human mind"; and lastly, if there is a good deal of truth mixed up with tradition.

According to M. Bergson, the chief characteristic of a primary intuition of this kind is that it begins with a negation. The first word formed in the mind of a philosopher should be the word *impossible*, as in the reason of Socrates arguing with his demon. This is obvious, for one only affirms to guard oneself from doubt, and the most dangerous and formidable form of doubt is that which takes the form of an error.

In the present case, it is easy to find the primary negation. St. Thomas was aware of the double position, taken by the Averroists, and previously countenanced by Abelard: as believers we affirm, as philosophers we deny or dispute. Even St. Anselm had betrayed some confusion on the respective scope, principles, and methods of faith and reason. St. Thomas was, moreover, convinced that, despite the great value of the Augustinian philosophy, it was incapable of answering the problems of contemporary thought. Therefore, he began over again. It was impossible that there should be any incompatibility, contradiction, or confusion between reason and faith. They must both be defended and brought into harmony. It was impossible for the Platonic philosophy of Augustine to remedy the ills caused by the new intellectual movement. The much-suspected Aristotelianism could furnish a remedy, provided it was corrected and brought into line with faith, and with what there was of truth in the other systems. That, in brief, was to be the life work of St. Thomas.

The first thing to be done was to insist on the autonomy and independence of both faith and reason; to give each its rights, and allow each to develop according to its own laws. Without that, any attempt at harmony would be special pleading. We cannot be said to reconcile two things if we allow either of them to suffer in any degree, yet that was precisely what had been done. Theology, in the preceding centuries, had had exclusive dominion, and a pure philosophy like Aristotle's was, in certain quarters, looked upon as a scandal. The school of St. Augustine held that all philosophical speculation was derived from, and depended upon, faith; in other words, they did not believe in a philosophy that was autonomous. The well-known phrase *fides quaerens intellectum*[13] sums up their position. Faith, they held, seeks to understand, but it remains faith for all that. It may be illustrated by reason, but it does not thereby lose its proper nature. While St. Thomas, it is true, admitted this principle and used it as much as anyone else, he did not consider it a complete expression of the work that had to be done. Reason also has its rights, its own province, its own methods, and its own certitudes, and its systematic treatment is not only man's privilege, but his bounden duty.

The remedy certainly did not consist in pouring some philosophy, so to speak, into theology, or reason into faith; nor even in "reconciling" them, as we reconcile people who have incompatible views, yet are forced to live together. St. Thomas did not set out to readjust them by making concessions to both sides, or by sacrificing the one for the other; that would have been work

[13] "Faith seeking understanding."

thrown away. No, he had to crown each of them sovereign in its own realm; to acknowledge the rights, albeit distinct and unequal, that belonged to each. Then he could attempt to harmonize them.

It was treason to give up an article of faith in favor of reason, but, in his eyes, it was just as bad to give up reason for the faith. Indeed, the treason was fundamentally the same in each case — namely, treason against God, the living Truth. In the Church and in nature, in revelation and in the human mind, God is one and the same. True reconciliation could be brought about only by holding fast to this principle and by an unwavering insistence on the respective claims of both faith and reason. Truth must agree with truth.

This desire to give equal honor to the believer and to the philosopher shows a remarkably bold and noble attribute of mind. If faith is divine, why distrust reason? There can be no danger to faith in the study of philosophy, once granted that they have the same origin, and must therefore be in accord. God cannot contradict himself, nor is he jealous of the creature's intellectual yearnings.

St. Thomas was determined to be neither arrogant in matters of faith, nor timid in matters of reason. He insists on the entire rights of each; he is theologian and philosopher, and these two sciences seemed to him, as M. Pierre Lasserre puts it, "two zones in the path of one and the same ray of heavenly wisdom."

On the other hand, he did not regard philosophy as completely cut off from faith, or entirely independent of it. That would destroy the unity of truth, the unity of man, and, we may almost say, the unity of God. It would also be ignoring the fact that the relation of God and creature in faith is very different from the relation of God and creature in reason. In faith, God reveals himself directly and infallibly. In reason, he reveals himself indirectly, in the sense that he possesses the *reasons* of things and gives the creature the intellect whereby these things are known. But human reason is weak, and where its conclusions do not agree with faith, it must be abandoned in favor of the infallible truth.

But it is nonetheless true that, if nothing be affirmed as of faith which is not of faith, or as proved by reason, when it is only a hypothesis or a fallacy, then all conflict between the two is ruled out, and each is free to develop. We may defend dogma with the weapons of reason, or illustrate philosophy by faith, without compromising either of them, or confusing them. It is possible in this way to be at once the most orthodox theologian and the most rational of philosophers. This must not be taken to imply that we claim to demonstrate the truths of faith, as Abelard and even Anselm tried to do. St. Thomas considered such procedure as lowering the dignity of faith and making it the laughing-stock of philosophers. What we can do, however, is to bring each into harmony with the other, and both with experience, and to refute all objections against faith, seeing that they must of necessity be invalid.

All through his life, this was St. Thomas's point of view. He was never merely a philosopher; he was *Doctor Catholicus* and theologian. But he was master in every department of truth. Having once bowed down his intelligence before God, he proudly defends its supremacy over all other truth. He makes it the handmaid of faith where he should, but queen in its own domain. Where this first homage is refused, reason soon comes even to doubt itself, as we see whenever there is a crisis in faith, and when the intellect rebels. When God has been ousted and reason made a god, reason has no remedy for its obvious weakness. It begins to doubt its own validity, and then there is nothing left. Humility, which emphasizes the due order of all things, is the greatest safeguard for the intellect, as for every other faculty.

There is every reason why the philosopher should make use of the data of faith for his own guidance and profit. There is no contradiction involved in using one science to direct and control another. There is no confusion between a branch and its flower; taken separately, they might differ in many respects, but taken together, they harmonize perfectly.

In the same way, the Thomist uses reason and faith, without confusing either them or their methods. In philosophy, he uses only philosophical arguments and deduces his conclusions from principles common to all things; therefore, these conclusions cannot be, properly speaking, *disbelieved*. If they could be proven false, the believer and the philosopher would fall together; but if they cannot be impugned, then both triumph together, by the action of one and the same intelligence. In order to light up a dark room, it is not necessary to shut out the natural light of day. Indeed, while firmly upholding the essential distinction between faith and reason, we have every right to endorse this daring proposition of John Scotus Erigena: "True religion is true philosophy; true philosophy is true religion."

This broad principle, which he keeps on reiterating and is forever defending from attacks of all kinds, he now set himself to apply. He had two things to do. First, he had to show that, between faith and reason, in *fact* as well as in theory, there is no contradiction, even though faith surpasses reason. Therefore, none of the objections raised by philosophy can be really valid, however difficult they may be to answer. This was the more important part of his plan, since it was an attempt to save Christian society, and he set to work with an ardor equaled only by his loyalty. It may be said that he left very little for the unbeliever of the future to do, since he made a point of stressing, not only the truth, but all the pros and cons of the problems under discussion.

St. Thomas is fond of saying that the philosopher's work *par excellence* is *order*. Having established a theoretical conformity between faith and reason, his second task was therefore to arrange the data of faith (which are naturally systematic, since they come from God) in as strict an order as possible, and then to construct a synthesis that would include them and the data of experience or acquired knowledge. He strove to create, not merely a system of dogmas, not merely a philosophy or a science, but a complete synthesis of knowledge, in which everything would find a place, and be related with everything else: "the hymn of the relations of all things," to borrow a phrase from Mallarmé. It was an ideal and, therefore, could not be fully realized. He wished to found what we may call a divine humanism; he wished to connect sound common sense to sublime dogma, by a wide road traversing all degrees of speculative thought. He wished to explain Christianity intellectually, and to Christianize intellectual thought. He envisaged the world, philosophically as a network of causes and effects, and theologically as a receptacle of divine thoughts and divine intentions. His task was to "determine which was which, and set them in motion," as Pascal would say. He grappled with this task until he exhausted his strength; he spent all his vitality and mental energy in the cause of truth, for which alone he lived and prematurely died.

Descartes, Malebranche, Leibnitz, and others have tried to form a similar system of Christian philosophy that would show forth the conformity of faith and reason. Although they did not entirely fail, it is quite certain that none of them met with a degree of success comparable with that which attended St. Thomas. What is more, some of these sincere attempts have ended by going against their very principles. Descartes's harmony has produced Spinoza and Bayle, and prepared the way for Voltaire. Not that

Descartes can be held responsible for these, but — by their fruits ye shall know them.

Now, why was Aristotle's philosophy chosen as the basis of this great reform? Certainly not because St. Thomas wished to be in the fashion and to follow the new learning, which he had so often to confute. Albert the Great undoubtedly influenced him, in the sense that he finally convinced him, but all through his studies, and especially in his debates, the idea had been gradually taking hold of him, and we have a right to ask why.

There was one general incentive, which appealed even to the religious authorities, despite their misgivings about Aristotle. They saw that it was necessary to capture for the Church this splendid revival of learning, which was everywhere making its presence felt. Ever since the fleshpots of Egypt, the true religion has consistently pursued a like policy. Historians such as Harnack, and indeed, writers of any real insight, have noticed this remarkable fact. Barrès writes, "One of the most striking facts in history is the way in which Christianity, having once definitely conquered, stays the hand of the would-be iconoclasts and says: Now that our enemy is down, we may take from him whatever good he may possess."[14] There have been intellectual iconoclasts as well, and the Church has always checked them in the same way. There were plenty such in St. Thomas's day. Albert the Great roundly denounced them, not sparing members of his own order: "They are mere brutes *(bruta animalia)* who blaspheme what they do not know." St. Thomas himself would have no truck with them. He is a Christian, but antiquity was also Christian, in the sense that all truth is

[14]Maurice Barrès, *Les Maitres*, Dante.

Christian, and it was the Church's right and the Christian's duty to take over whatever good it contained. Those rather too daring words of Péguy, which are often given a bad meaning, can be understood in a quite orthodox sense by the Thomist: "I wish to be a Christian, but I wish also to be pagan."

This was to be a reconciliation of the Gospels and Greek philosophy, of faith and reason, of revelation and natural genius, under the inspiration of Aristotle. Thought was to be unified: past and present united.

What made this unification more feasible was the fact that, whereas the ancient philosophies were all more or less deficient, Aristotelianism appeared to St. Thomas an incomparable masterpiece; a thoughtful system, and so adaptable as to give the impression of being sound good sense exalted by genius. It was searching enough to reach the precise position that the mind should take up in order to furnish a complete solution to all problems of a serious nature. It was comprehensive enough to include any lawful additions and any reasonable interpretation, and, for this purpose, was supremely synthetical. It was like an encyclopedia in the making, which could be extended in every way. It followed the laws of organic development, which always makes the fullest use of what it absorbs, without destroying the harmony of the whole.

It would be a great triumph to show how the dogmatic teaching of the Church could be expressed in terms of this philosophy and defended by it. It would be a grand victory that would secure a vast treasure and would avert the impending danger of the two doctrines drifting ever further apart, losing touch one with the other, and finally breaking out into open war, with harmful consequences to souls.

It was his great heart that gave St. Thomas the confidence he needed; the great heart of a believer, animated by a twofold faith, the faith of a Christian, and his faith, with which six years of intense study had imbued him, in the greatest of all purely human philosophies. He was confident from the start that this synthesis, however difficult, could be made, and he succeeded. We of today will appreciate his task, if we agree with the writer who says of Aristotle that he was "perhaps the only ancient who would have been a modern."

It was imperative, however, not to mistake, still less to ignore, the relative values of the two sciences. Revealed truth must be put first, as the supreme rule of all Christians. Reason must be the handmaid of faith, and not *vice versa.* It was not a question of making faith tally with Aristotle, but of defining it in the philosophical language of Aristotle, whose teaching was, presumably, equally true.

Medieval paintings represent this subjugation of Aristotle to the faith in a rather crude manner, but they do at least bring out the fact that his subjugation in no way impaired his freedom of investigation, or denied his autonomy in his own sphere. In what is known as the *Lay of Aristotle* and is believed to refer to the story of Campaspe, the knight on horseback represents the new theology riding on philosophy, rather like the window at Chartres where St. Matthew, representing the New Testament, is riding on Isaiah, representing the Old. Now, just as St. Matthew's divine mission does not belittle that of Isaiah, so the truth of faith does not damage the autonomy of philosophy.

We must not, however, forget the complementary truth contained in the following extract from a sermon preached by St. Thomas before the University of Naples: "Any old woman today knows more about things divine than did all the philosophers of antiquity put together." Aristotle was to be made to serve, but without restricting his freedom of inquiry; truth is never shackled by becoming the handmaid of truth.

The sequel will show that this was a hazardous venture, and had St. Thomas sought peace and quiet, he would have done better to have tried some other means. But adventure is the lot of all heroes, not excluding heroes of thought.

Aristotle was to be "corrected," not in the sense that any of his fundamental principles were to be rejected, but in the sense that they were to be more thoroughly investigated, and, with the guidance of faith, to be brought to their logical conclusions. If Aristotle had come to life again in the thirteenth century, he would have found this follower more Aristotelian than he had himself been, because he was going more deeply into his principles and applying them to correct incidental error.

St. Thomas adopted Aristotle's principles as a kind of framework. Although, to all appearances, he accepted the Aristotelian world as it stood, he really transformed it basically by fitting into it such notions as creation, providence, free will, and miracles. Yet this is still Aristotle, only a better version of him, being more logically developed and nearer the truth. "Aristotle's greatest achievement," says Emile Boutroux, "is the Christian philosophy." And the Christian philosophy of today is the philosophy of St. Thomas.

One other important fact, which helps us to realize St. Thomas's greatness, was that he took over Aristotle's philosophy at the point where it parts company with Plato's, and not at a much later point where it becomes identified with the philosophies of his first disciples, who soon lapsed into naturalism. Plato was more religious than Aristotle, and St. Thomas had to combine the learning of the one with the religious spirit of the other.

But the Plato that he knew was hardly the real Plato, whose works were then little known, but Plato as found in the Fathers, and especially in St. Augustine. He, in a sense, pitted the Augustinian philosophy against its followers. But his system was balanced and coherent, and he regarded this Platonism, which was essential to theology, only as supplementary to philosophy. He interpreted St. Augustine in an Aristotelian sense, and Aristotle in an Augustinian sense. He discarded Augustine only where he was too Platonic, and Aristotle only where he was not sufficiently Christian. Thus, he avoided both extremes and built up a Christian Aristotelianism, animated by Platonism and tinged with the Neo-Platonism of the School of Alexandria.

We have just said that St. Thomas was forced to disclaim the naturalism of Aristotle, as developed by one school of followers, which departed from his principles and cut itself off entirely from the Platonic element in his philosophy. This must be understood to refer to that extreme form of naturalism which excludes all spiritual realities. In a different sense, St. Thomas was an ardent naturalist, because he found there a remedy for the baneful effects of false mysticism or unscientific spirituality, which was then, as always, a real menace.

We glibly criticize him for not paying sufficient attention to physics, and to the physical nature of man. Read superficially, he seems to merit this criticism, because of the kind of questions that he treats, and because he was a theologian before all else. But it is a criticism that has no solid foundation, especially when examined historically. He found in Aristotle a deep interest in nature, and a man of his common sense readily assimilated it. He taught that grace builds upon nature, and, in general, he makes the spiritual world the continuation and crown of the corporeal. Hence his oft-repeated axioms, that grace does not destroy nature but perfects it, and that the soul, despite its spiritual character, cannot be completely defined without the body. The soul is the form of the body, and grace is the supernatural form of the soul. As a pyramid has its base on the ground and its apex tending heavenward, so the Thomistic system unites the natural philosophy of Aristotle with the supernatural doctrine of God.

It was not St. Thomas, but the Augustinians and Neo-Platonists, his predecessors and contemporaries, who were so wrapped up in things divine and in man's relations with God as to lose sight of the relations of God with material things, and the soul's relations with the body. Not that they were positively wrong, but they were narrow, and something quite revolutionary was needed to broaden their outlook.

This, then, was St. Thomas's plan. First formed before he left Cologne, it took more definite shape as he worked at it, for the blurred details in the conception of a plan are always brought into focus by its execution.

We must insist, especially in a book of this kind, that his constructive ability, which seems so impersonal and cold, was really the outcome of a great yearning. He longed to know, for his own sake, the answer to the question of his childhood: *What is God?* And he longed to spread this knowledge; to live up to the motto of his order: *Contemplata aliis tradere.*

Every great philosophy must bear a moral character, not only because it must treat of ethics, but also in its very inspiration and spirit. This is particularly true of Thomism. It would be but poorly understood and misrepresented if we dwelt merely on its questions and replies and its rigid logic. There is a great undercurrent of spirituality, the outflowing of a deep and ardent thinker who devoted his life to an attempt at finding out the true meaning of life.

What is first in order of execution is not, in this case, first in order of conception. It is not the principles that are our first concern.

We must go deeper than his teaching if we are to discover his real attitude; we must look where he reveals his heart as well as his mind.

We may not unfittingly apply to him the definition that Dante consecrates to God: "an intellectual light full of love."[15] He tackled these problems, not out of curiosity or ambition, but because they were of importance to mankind. To his superb intelligence was joined the faith of a simple child. While his task might justifiably have monopolized his talents, he was ever ready to use them for others. He thought in order to live himself and to help others to live. He sought to find his way about the world, that he might walk in it and help us to walk. He studied everything to find out the meaning of our existence and subordinated all things to the last end, where they find their true explanation.

It was fortunate that these times had a man sufficiently farseeing to discover what was needed, and sufficiently able and generous to satisfy that need. Barrès says that "a genius is one who can give us what we need, when nobody else can do it."[16] St. Thomas, of his own accord, shepherded the wandering flock, lest it be said that, by withholding his help, he had allowed it to perish.

Et que, faute d'un coeur, un siècle soit perdu.[17] — Lamartine

[15] Dante, *Divine Comedy*, "Paradise," canto 30, line 40.

[16] Barrès, *Les Maitres*, Dante.

[17] "And that, for lack of one heart, the century was lost."

Chapter Four

St. Thomas's Method

In imitation of the well-known book entitled *Introduction to the Method of Leonardo da Vinci*, we might head this chapter "Introduction to the Method of St. Thomas Aquinas." Here are some of its principal characteristics.

Unlike so many who start a work without first attending to their own formation, as if the two were unconnected, St. Thomas began with himself. Our action is our second act. He wished his work to be fruitful, useful, and edifying, so he began by forming his own character, knowing that it would color not only the spiritual, but also the technical and intellectual, character of his writings. In philosophy, in theology, and in science, his method was to be the method of sanctity.

He was distinguished first and foremost for his power of intellect, which, in him, was not so much a particular trait, as the very essence of his life. It gave a unity to his whole life: it was his profession as Doctor, while in his preaching, he only simplified and elaborated his doctrine and adapted it to the exigences of the pulpit. In his poetry, he sings in concepts; his mysticism is intellectual rather than emotional. Even his prayers are didactic in form, like the articles in the *Summa*, which are really quite as spiritual, although not so obviously so.

His task was to see and then to show others what he had seen. Therefore, he had first to rectify his outlook. He who would speak wisely must behave wisely.

It is a great mistake to imagine that we think only with our brain. We think with our whole being and, more particularly, with our whole soul, and it is the various inclinations of the soul that lead us toward or away from the truth, that make us prejudiced, or our judgements biased and capricious.

Pasteur wanted somebody to write a book on the influence of the heart in the progress of knowledge. It would certainly account for a great deal: we know what is meant in Scripture by purity of heart. Truth does not change, but the angle from which we view it is governed by our general attitude, and, if that is wrong, then our keenness of sight is only an additional danger.

Again, to see without bias calls for a certain detachment from other things. To be in the right atmosphere for knowledge, one must make heroic sacrifices, and, if knowledge is one's sole aim, everything else must be laid aside. "Every conquest of learning," writes Nietzsche, "is the outcome of our own courage and austerity."

Philosophy, like art, implies of its nature a detachment from concrete reality and a quest of ideal sources, or causes, and it is not surprising that St. Thomas's power was enhanced by his retiring disposition, and by that detachment from things which resulted from his vows. His loyalty to truth was due as much to his complete disinterestedness as to his right-mindedness. He was able to forget himself, so absorbed was he in his thought; he was ready to identify his fate with that of the truth, as a miser will sacrifice all in his greed for gold.

Rodin made a curious experiment. He found that he could change the word *Jesus* to *sculpture* whenever it occurred in the *Imitation of Christ*, and every passage remained true. This only shows that technical work requires the same conditions as sanctity, and that the holier a man is, the better is his work. St. Thomas's moral attitude was possibly due to some similar reflection. We might apply to him those words addressed to the Tree of Knowledge in the *Ebauche d'un Serpent:*

> *Grand être agité de savoir,*
> *Qui toujours, comme pour mieux voir,*
> *Grandis à l'appel de ta cime.*[18]

St. Thomas strove to make his holiness keep pace with his learning, that he might have a clearer perception of reality. Just as the Beatific Vision is the reward of virtue, so understanding is the combined product of holiness and natural talent. Holiness is a necessary condition, although not, of course, the only one. Indeed, learning, according to St. Thomas, is simply one of the forms under which holiness acts; it is holiness using natural talents, to witness to the truth, and spending itself to make truth reign supreme.

With these views, it was only natural that he should join an order whose motto is Truth. There, doubtless, he expected to find the intellectual resources he desired. But a religious order is not a school: it has vows that are essential to it, and it was in them that St. Thomas found what his intellect required. By thus giving himself to God, he became detached, unburdened, and settled. He

[18] I am grateful to Fr. John O'Connor for the following translation: "Great nature, quivering to know, / Evermore spreading up, as though / For wider view to thy crown wouldst grow."

gave up external goods by his vow of poverty and could now forget his gentle birth, having nothing to administer, nothing to answer for, and, above all, nothing to expect. Henceforth, he will handle only intangible truths; he will covet, not the miser's gold or the vanities of this world, but the light of truth.

His having been girt by angels he regarded as a token of God's will, and in matters of purity, he ever remained as a "child of five." Men of the world may be inclined to scoff at his lack of experience of human passions, which his ascetism suggests, but his writings give the lie to this. Even a pagan like Plato knew that "vice can know neither itself nor virtue, but virtue can know both itself and vice." In the midst of troubles of the flesh, with its ever-changing desires, madness, deceit, and remorse, which sap our mental energy and impede our intellectual pursuits, who can possibly reason clearly?

By the vow of obedience, St. Thomas simplified his life by giving up all responsibility other than his work, and even that he thereby made to depend on God's providential design, rather than on his own will.

To the vows, he added certain virtues that seem to follow from them. By his humility, he forsook honors and disdained flattery. To borrow a phrase from Pascal, "he sought inspiration through humiliations," and he was able to say of himself that he never remembered giving way to a temptation to vainglory. Mortification enabled him to neglect the care of his body, to practice strict fasting and abstinence, especially when a difficulty troubled him. He did not, however, practice the extreme penances that were customary in his age, as he judged them to be detrimental to his work. Silence, "the father of preachers," and solitude particularly become a deep thinker, who must listen when wisdom is speaking. All great achievements are done in a silence "higher than the stars, and deeper than the realms of the dead." He was detached even in his work, because he concentrated on his proper object, and ignored all extraneous matters. This was a real sacrifice, for he had a natural aptitude for all branches of learning, and he had to pass them by unexplored. "A wise man," says Goethe, "avoids all distracting knowledge; he specializes in one branch and masters it." This must not be taken too literally, for every particular study implies a wider knowledge: true perspective needs a broad outlook. But St. Thomas always avoided knowledge that was distracting. At Paris, St. Louis once asked his advice on certain questions that he intended to discuss in court on the morrow. He answered them as well as he could, but with brevity and without really rising to the occasion. For, although "when he applied his mind to affairs of this world, he judged them with a wisdom which to everyone seemed divine" (as an old biographer says), still, he did not consider this a sufficient motive for making a thorough study of them.

With these virtues to help him, St. Thomas became as adept in learning as man, by his own power, can be. There was now no obstacle between the mind and its object. Pride, vanity, and ambition warp the intelligence and make it partial and intellectually callous. He was passive, in the sense that there was nothing arbitrary about his philosophy: it was not the result of a personal *fiat*, but was imposed by the inexorable necessity of things. He was, as it were, the hub of converging forces.

This made it harder for him, because an ideal reconstruction of the world offers less scope than does the recognition of it as it is. The imaginative use fable; the hard-working use history. As Marcel Proust remarks, "All mental action is easy so long as it is not tied down to reality." To be tied down to reality implies a detachment from self, and from the thousand and one artifices of fancy and caprice. St. Thomas's sound judgment is remarkable as much for its justice as for its justness. He respected the rights of things and of other people's views. He had very little of that curious tendency, common to all of us, to believe the man who is always right, the man who sets himself up as judge of everything and who laughs superciliously at the stupidity around him. His very objectivity demanded that he should retire from this topsy-turvy world of passions and small talk, and from the material world of everyday needs. He asked nothing of the world but to be its servant, and to lead it to the truth.

There is one still more important point about his method. It was useless to detach himself from the world, if he were not thereby to receive something, to be richer, to be able to give. He did not work for a negative result or merely for himself. Truth is living and is never entirely subdued save by love; it is the common heritage of mankind, and nobody has any right to monopolize it. Moreover, there is a sprinkling of truth in the opinions of all men, and we must collect it before we can pass it on. Now this can be done only by sympathy, which establishes contact with others. As St. Albert the Great says, "Let us be two, but let the cause be one."

St. Thomas made God the center of his doctrine; he set out to know God, his relation to creatures, and the creatures' relations to him. That, since, in fact, it includes everything, was his entire object. Spinoza would not have been far wrong in making all things either God or modes of God, had he at the same time recognized God's transcendence.

This concentration of everything in God did not consist in a simple coordination in logic, as might be made by a clever logician.

No, God was the center in a more vital way; the center of his contemplation and love and, hence, of his experience and intuition; he was not merely a concept. His contemporaries, who were best able to know, affirm that in his exposition of doctrine all his syllogisms were the outcome of a genius that was to a great extent intuitive and supernatural — in short, of a gift.

There are, he tells us, two ways of approaching God, which usually go hand in hand:

> To be able to judge of things divine, by human reasoning, belongs to the intellectual virtue of wisdom . . . But there is another "wisdom descending from above" . . . by which we judge of them, by being, as it were, raised to a state connatural to theirs. This wisdom is the gift of the Holy Ghost, and it perfects a man by making him not only learn, but also experience the things of God.[19]

He says very much the same thing in his commentary on St. Paul's words: "He who is joined to the Lord is one spirit."[20]

Reason brings God within our compass, but it is an intermediary; by love, on the other hand, we possess him intimately and share his secrets. And if genius be joined to the love, it will establish a reciprocal relation, similar to the relation between a work and the inspiration that created it, as explained by Goethe. Genius is like the shuttle that draws the woof through the warp and thereby weaves the cloth.

All his biographers agree that St. Thomas sought in prayer and contemplation, and even in ecstasy, the intuitions that he then put into the scholastic form of theorems and *scholia*, for teaching

[19] *Summa Theologica*, II-II, Q. 14, arts. 1, 2.

[20] 1 Cor. 6:17.

purposes. He tells us himself that he learned more at the foot of the crucifix than from books. He would put his head against the tabernacle to discover its secrets, like a little child. At Mass and Compline, he often wept, and he asked with tears the answers to his abstract questions. Knowledge for him was a sort of pilfering from heaven: he knew that the vast stream of knowledge must ultimately have its rise in God.

From the very start, his vocation was not to be intellectual only; he was to be espoused to the living Truth. He who possessed being, in abstract form, was to be possessed by Being. His intellectual as well as his practical life was to be governed by this surrender of his own being, and having thus attained intimacy with God, he would find in God whereby to become intimate with everything else.

The same may be said of his attitude toward other philosophers. He was sympathetic enough to make their wisdom his own, by understanding their position and taking what there was of good in them. He thus became a contemporary of all antiquity, a worker in the present, and hence a prophet of the future.

Nor are the vocations of intellect and love really distinct, for God, the source of things, is equally the source of the thought in which things are reflected. "All truth is from the Holy Spirit." This was a sufficient reason for trying to understand other people's thought, collaborating with them, and using their discoveries.

When one's purpose is to give rather than to receive, this method of love makes one ready and eager to spend oneself in the cause, obedient to superiors, the representatives of God, and prompt to comply with requests of any kind. These are signs of God's will, and by being thus prepared to obey, we satisfy the two precepts of loving God and our neighbor, which, according to St. Thomas, are really one and the same precept.

A truly great man has a certain right to be an egoist. His egoism is for the general good, provided it is prudently controlled. It must, then, be an act of boundless generosity when such a one gives away all, his work and his very being.

St. Thomas did not map out his life and choose his work. His teaching and practically all his writings were done at the command of his superiors, or at the request of his fellow-religious or others. He felt that he would be doing a more useful work by using his knowledge to answer occasional inquiries than if all his work had been carefully arranged for him according to a strictly logical plan. After all, these chance occurrences were just as truly from God as any regular daily round of work.

According to St. Augustine, the highest form of charity is that of teaching, while St. Thomas extols the gift of truth above every other. He agreed with Plato that error is more harmful than homicide and that error due to negligence, or error about things that it is our duty to study, is as bad as murder.

It was reflections of this kind that led him to attempt a task so arduous that he died prematurely, a martyr to truth. He cut out of his life all that was foreign to his purpose: the athlete must run clad as lightly as possible. He simply thought. He would never allow himself even the most harmless distractions or friendships, that might in any way impede his work. He said Mass early each morning, heard another as his thanksgiving, and often served it, and then betook himself to his work, which often went on far into the night.

At table he had to be watched, because he neglected the needs of the body, so engrossed was he in his thoughts. When others tried to get him to recreate or take a walk in the garden, he would go with a smile, but return to his cell at the first opportunity. "The well-used cell becomes sweet," says the *Imitation of Christ*. But it was the inner sanctuary of the soul that he guarded with special care, hearing only when appealed to, and speaking only in reply to others.

He worked quickly but without undue haste, perhaps with some forebodings of the fewness of his days. Yet he never worried about the completion of his work, knowing that God would take it up where he dropped it, if only he did God's will.

He never allowed his studies to interfere with his proper profession of preaching. His sermons, as those which have survived testify, were didactic, but it would be unfair to conclude from these notes and skeleton sermons that he was an uninteresting preacher. After all, the writings of St. Vincent Ferrer or Savonarola make equally dull reading. A magistrate bore witness at his canonization that, at Naples, St. Thomas was interrupted by the tears of the congregation. He never, however, preached for effect: his manner was calm and without gesticulations, with his eyes upcast as if in a sort of ecstasy. He seems to have impressed his hearers rather as Newman did, by his deep sincerity and his penetrating voice.

St. Thomas put these principles into practice in his very method of teaching. His love of God naturally led him to adopt the synthetic method, or the reassembling of scattered truths into a unified whole. Synthesis is a law of all art, but it belongs in a special way to metaphysics, which traces, in abstract language, the fundamental relations of all things. St. Thomas's design was simply to take everything into account. False systems are false only insofar as they neglect some aspect of reality; they sin by defect. A true system must be complete and must therefore probe every problem and examine every opinion, to find out exactly what these opinions have in common.

Since all things come from God, they must be in reality united, and therefore somehow reconcilable in the opinions of men. Relative truth must ultimately lead to absolute truth, and there is no statement in science that is not relatively true. Pure error cannot be put into words, much less can it gain adherents. "The false," says St. Thomas, "is true in a certain sense." The investigation of an error will lead to what gave rise to it, from which it derives its apparent truth and cogency, and that must be a truth of some sort. This basic truth, reached after endless soundings, and the substratum of all thought, can be used to reconcile contrary statements, when they can be reconciled, and to judge and refute them when they are incompatible. This method is positive even where it is critical, and constructive even where it appears to destroy.

Truth, then, is to be found everywhere, and in every age. St. Thomas did not study tradition, as some have done, to pull it to pieces, and form a new system that should do without it. He was not like Kant, who wished to form "an entirely new science, which nobody had ever thought of before"; nor was he like Descartes, who "did not even wish to know whether anybody had lived before him." Such an impossible attitude points to the complete stagnation of philosophic thought. Truth belongs to every generation, and a lover of truth must be the contemporary of all ages: he must be already venerable, if he wishes to be abreast of the times. One must be disciple before master, and the greatest innovator is he who borrows most from the wisdom of the ages. Because of the peculiar character of his work, St. Thomas felt that he could not afford to pass over any author, just as a good builder will look about everywhere for his materials.

He paid special attention to the great works of genius, because they contained a larger quota of truth, whether original or second-hand. He was quite impartial. He studied principally the Fathers of the Church, and, in the words of Leo XIII, "for having venerated them, he inherited the learning of them all." But he read a good many others as well, especially the philosophers. He was conversant with the historians, lawyers, doctors, orators, poets, grammarians, and geographers of antiquity. He quotes, among others, Ovid, Horace, Caesar, Cicero, Seneca, Terence, Sallust, Livy, Strabo, Valerius Maximus, Galen, and Hippocratus. He was familiar with works of Arab and Jewish philosophy, while he made a profound study of the old theologians. He undoubtedly knew some of these at secondhand, through Albert the Great, who was widely read.

He studied the past, not to save himself the trouble of thinking, but to prepare the ground; he discovered his own position and true orientation by comparison with what these others had already done. Tradition supplied the stimulus rather than the substance of his thought.

There are numerous well-known passages in which he gives his views about borrowing from other writers. The following are from his commentary on the *Metaphysics*:

> In the investigation of truth, one person is helped by another in two ways, one direct, the other indirect. Directly, one is helped by those who have already discovered the truth, because each earlier writer has found some part of it. When these parts are assembled, later writers are led to a greater knowledge of truth. Indirectly one is helped insofar as those who have erred in the past have given their followers a chance of vindicating the truth more clearly, by searching criticism.[21]

[21] Bk. 2, lect. 1.

> Just as nobody can give a fair judgement without hearing the arguments for both sides, so he who studies philosophy judges the better, if he hears all the arguments of those who call it in question.[22]

So insistent is St. Thomas on this principle that he might be accused of not practicing what he preached, were it not that his sole object was doctrine. He is not always accurate as a historian of philosophy. He is not much interested in whether an author thought this or that. He is in search of the truth, and, if he believes that he has found it in some text, as *he* understands it, or as he thinks it ought to be understood, he quotes it, without troubling very much to find out whether the meaning that he gives it is exactly what the author intended it to mean. Elsewhere he commentates on what the author meant to say rather than on what he actually says. This is hardly exact criticism, but it is an indication that his sole object was to find out the truth and pass it on to others.

Deep interest in profane writers can hardly be said to have been common in his day. Many theologians considered it useless and dangerous to pursue studies that were not theological — the Bible, the Fathers, and the approved Doctors they considered quite enough, while the study of nature and the humanities that flourished in antiquity were excluded as too worldly.

St. Thomas thought otherwise; he was a humanist in the best sense of the word. He failed to see how the study of God's handiwork, in itself and as reflected in these writers, could possibly harm our knowledge of God, seeing that this knowledge is, in part, derived from nature and is always illuminated and corroborated by

[22] Bk. 3, lect. 1.

nature. The world is an effect of God, and no true study of it can lead us away from its Author. The world is a commentary on God's Word and moves as to admire his wisdom and adore his bounty.

While it is true that human learning may lead to pride, it does not follow that to be humble we must be ignorant. Great learning, once safeguarded from hindering sanctity, becomes a powerful aid to it. The greater a man, the greater the need of humility since only as little children can we enter the kingdom of heaven. But once a man has conquered his pride and is on the right road, his superior learning assists him, rather as powerful headlights assist the motorist.

St. Thomas held that the profane sciences could be studied in a Christian spirit: nature could be made divine; philosophy and the natural sciences could be used in conjunction with theology properly so called. He resolved to treat, not only of God's relations with everything else, but also of the relations of everything with God. God was to be the center of a universal knowledge, with radiations in every direction; a synthesis comprising God and "all human ideas, synthesized at their base by sound reasoning, and at their summit by sound faith."

Another effect of this exclusive love of truth was his sense of proportion. He never exaggerates; he is never partial; he never pushes an idea to the detriment of others that happen to be less original or less brilliant. Other systems make a fetish of certain notions, while they neglect or belittle all others, but violence of this sort is incompatible with truth. Truth has no favorites: everything must be weighed on a sensitive balance, and nothing may be sacrificed; all things must be in proportion and judged on their merits.

A true philosopher must give every truth its due, no matter how insignificant it may seem.

St. Thomas would have endorsed the remark of Nietzsche, that "every reality is, of its nature, an object of respect." There is no room for undue emphasis when the entire truth can be viewed from different angles and when every truth, precisely as such, is regarded as of equal value. Exaggeration implies a failure to grasp the true relations of things and a sacrifice of the whole in favor of some of its parts.

A philosophical thesis can be better explained than by exaggerating it at the expense of other theses. St. Thomas would compare it with the others, concentrate all his knowledge on that point, and thereby find its exact significance. No matter what element of reality he might be treating, he marshals the whole of his philosophy in support. It is often a matter of surprise to find him advancing great fundamental principles in support of an insignificant thesis. Just as a vulture describes great circles before it drops onto a field-mouse, so he sets out from a universe to reach a tiny truth, because he is aware that in the "sphere whose center is everywhere, and whose circumference is nowhere," everything is of equal importance. This being his attitude, he has no need to stress certain points; he has simply to incorporate all things in one universal plan.

For this synthesis, he made use of correct classifications and clear-cut definitions, as being the most suitable means of determining the relative values of things and of uniting them in one harmonious whole. "The man who can divide and define," says Plato, "shall be for me as a God."

The philosopher's first duty is to establish order. St. Thomas was the sworn enemy of confused thought. It was because of this ability to classify and order, and to reconstruct what he had patiently analyzed, that Leibnitz attributed to him a special gift of elucidating obscure problems. He avoids subtleties; he simplifies, and this by synthesis, not by mental juggling. His finished synthesis is like an engineer's plans, from which he or another might reconstruct a complicated piece of machinery.

Moreover, in agreement with the rule of Pascal, he never discussed a truth without taking into consideration the opposite truth. There are two sides to every question, and each may be legitimately weighed, developed, and possibly reconciled with the other. His mind, like that of his master Aristotle, oscillated between the pros and cons of a question, and finally dominated them all. Ideas that seemed to conflict when in shadow he showed to agree when brought into the full light of day.

Finally, what most characterizes his love of truth is his attitude toward his opponents. Indeed, he seems hardly to have opponents, so well does he work with them. St. Paul says, "Prove all things; hold fast that which is good."[23] To do this, we must first be able to recognize the good when we see it, and that implies sympathy. St. Thomas loved the truth that others possessed, because, as he says, "Truth does not change with the diversity of persons, and whoever maintains it is thereby invincible."[24] He dealt with his opponents not out of any vindictive desire to refute them, but rather to judge them fairly and meet them halfway. He accepts what is true in them, and rejects what is false, showing where it goes wrong.

As a small indication of this attitude, we may give the following: when he approves of an opinion, he quotes its author, but

[23] 1 Thess. 5:21.

[24] Commentary on Job, ch. 13, lect. 2.

when he condemns it, he simply refers to its author as *quidam*, "a certain one." It is a way of condoning the error, which, after all, is only a "lack of seeing the whole of a thing," as Pascal puts it. He defended his own teaching, not by being blind to all objections, but by a free discussion of the whole question. He therefore had no need to hold his opponents up to ridicule; he could praise them for the good they had accomplished and help to rectify their vision.

He was too discriminating to see only headstrongness and insincerity behind error. We are quite ready to claim a like indulgence for ourselves! He gave everyone his due, and, with strict impartiality, he rejected erroneous statements, even when they had the support of eminent men such as Aristotle, Augustine, or his own master, St. Albert. In his single-minded search for truth, he would accept the statement of an enemy and reject that of a friend.

The following fine passage of Kant would have met with his approval:

> The honor of human reason is, to some extent, vindicated by reconciling the diverse ideas of its greatest exponents, and by showing that, even when they are contradictory, they all contain some measure of truth.

Between all philosophies there is a latent connection, which it takes a profound thinker to discover. The common earth is below them as surely as the sky is above. Even a penetrating mind might hold false doctrine, but only because of the truth that it contains. Great antagonists are really much closer to each other than they imagine. They oppose and refute each other's arguments by invoking principles common to them both, and their antagonism has the effect of making them go more deeply into the matter, as in mining and countermining.

The true philosopher, and *a fortiori* the saint, must take his stand beside his adversaries, not opposite them. He must collaborate; he must use their true statements, and even their errors, to elucidate the truth. In a sense, he must be above truth and falsehood, and draw from both. Then will he experience the pleasures of discovery rather than the annoyance of controversy, since impartiality spells peace; it is only the temper that gets ruffled.

He felt acutely how mysterious everything was, and the more fundamental the question, the more diffident he became. The most fundamental question in philosophy is surely the validity of the principle of contradiction. Yet, in his opusculum *De Æternitate Mundi*, arguing with men who contested its validity, by granting God the power of acting against it, he simply answers with respectful reserve that that was not according to *his* way of thinking. It is well known that the human mind hesitates before such questions, and the deeper the question, the greater the hesitation. Great geniuses, trying to cope with these profundities, are like children groping in the dark.

When writing on points of doctrine, he usually expresses himself with more decision, but even here the careful reader will find that he makes use of all opinions, even those most opposed to his own. His synthesis was comprehensive enough to include them all; indeed, it had to include them all, for they each contained some aspect of truth not to be found elsewhere.

He seems in his element when dealing with ideas contrary to his own; he calmly steps over their pitfalls, and he derives more from a genius whose views are false than from a mediocre writer who is perfectly orthodox.

Again, he found that this study stimulated him and made him strengthen his position on those very points where so many fail. It is always profitable to converse with those whose errors are on vital points. Contradiction enriches our ideas, uncovers hidden pitfalls, and sharpens our wits. Goethe says, "What is like us, we may leave alone; it is what is opposed to us that stimulates us." When we go back to St. Thomas, after reading the maze of opinions put forward and discussed by his commentators, we realize that his brief expressions are as so many bridges over an abyss. The least change of word alters the sense, or obscures it. It was only by constant study of the errors that surrounded each doctrine that he was able to make a safe passage through. "Error is due to resemblance," says Plato. We must make a profound study of error to make sure that our truths do not resemble it, and do not thus deserve to be dubbed false.

So little did he fear opposition, that he set himself up as his own opponent and mustered the most formidable objections possible to his thesis. He was so confident that truth would triumph that he felt no uneasiness at attempts to undermine it. He puts forward the objections and the thesis with the same calmness, however sacred the subject, and appears to bestow the same care on each. It is extraordinary to see the calm way this saint sets snares for God, siding with atheists, agnostics, heretics, and pagans, more strongly than the most rabid of unbelievers. He is absolutely without fear, for he knows that the truth must escape every snare. He makes the Devil help him build a temple to God.

St. Thomas was able to relinquish his own opinions as readily as he absorbed those of others. He was ready to retract or amplify what he had said. He never, it is true, wrote a book of *Retractations*, as did St. Augustine, and the opusculum *De Concordantiis* found among his works is spurious, but he would retract on occasion, and that quite simply, without explanation or self-justification.

In short, St. Thomas is like the patriarch who "walks before God." In his thought, in his word, in his writings, his soul is untrammeled by personal motives and centered on truth. He is the interpreter of his poem of ideas; the hero of his book; the saint of the holiness he describes. His method was to unite wisdom and love in his studies and in his stewardship of the truth entrusted to him.

Chapter Five

The Genius of St. Thomas

Although all that we have said so far has been meant to throw light on the genius of St. Thomas, yet perhaps it will be as well to collect in a separate chapter its main characteristics.

Sheer intellectual greatness is never so attractive, never appeals so much to the imagination and to the emotions as greatness of a more practical kind. That is why Napoleon, Caesar, and Joan of Arc will always exercise a greater influence. Yet intellectual greatness must surely have a prior claim to nobility. "Man's whole dignity," says Pascal, "consists simply in thought." Hence, no influence can be more ennobling than the influence of St. Thomas.

It is not merely that he wins our admiration or even our ready allegiance; he overpowers us. Seldom has there been a person who has united such sureness, penetration, and breadth, who has been so well equipped to solve the riddle of the world, or to praise its Author.

His genius will stand the most formidable comparison. His intelligence was as vast as Aristotle's, as elevated as Plato's, and as acute as that of Socrates. And if due allowance be made for the difference of the ages in which they lived, his genius in every sphere, except that of mathematics, is as rich as that of Leibnitz. He soared as high as did St. Augustine, although in a different manner. Augustine had the wings of the eagle of St. John. St. Thomas had rather those of the lion of St. Mark, for, if his strength was leonine, the lion had wings.

He seems hardly so much a thinker, as one in whom thought operates of its own accord, without apparent effort, and without the laborious process evident in many great writers. "We feel," says Père Gratry of him, "that in his company we have leapt over worlds, and that thought no longer encumbers."

His acumen and deep learning equipped him for any intellectual pursuit. Speculation on the most profound matters was not the uphill work that it is for us.

We shall give the estimate of his contemporaries; that of posterity is familiar to all of us. Chroniclers who knew him well give us some striking details. He had an extraordinary power of concentrating, and, as we have seen, it served him as an effective anesthetic when he underwent surgical treatment. He composed long treatises mentally and dictated them at one sitting. Like Caesar, he could dictate to three or four scribes at once, and on different and always difficult matters. He would dictate in his sleep, or, at any rate, in a kind of sleep, when his body was unconscious and his mind fully awake. His memory, "which never forgot anything," stored up for him everything that he had ever learned, while his ceaseless application, his calmness, humility, and zeal, enabled him to compose a large number of treatises, even while he was working for others and carrying on controversies.

For us especially, who are considering his work, this aspect of his genius is interesting only as a curiosity; the main questions are, how did he use his powers, and what was the spiritual force behind them? In this respect, his most striking characteristics are his saneness, his simple straightforward manner, and his objectivity. One of his early disciples remarks that he was at once a Common Doctor *(Doctor Communis)* and an uncommon doctor, in that he followed the beaten path and discovered there truths that nobody had discovered before.

How many philosophical ideas owe their vogue to their provocativeness, to an undisciplined temperament, to a disregard of things as they really are! What Nietzsche calls "pure vision," vision free from all contingence and personal bias, like that of a pure spirit, is a rare phenomenon. St. Thomas had it. He knew truth instinctively, as an animal knows what is good for it, and we may follow him without fear of being led astray.

His method is always simple. The order of questions, and their treatment is never arbitrary, artificial, or "original." Everything follows from an ingenuous view of reality, and nature is not seen through a network of plausible concepts. It is true that he is not altogether free from the credulities and crudities of his age, but his sound sense saved him from much of the wasted dexterity, the absurdity and legend, that were then rife. He would not have been the great man he was, had he not been a little ahead of his contemporaries, and, like Saul, higher "from the shoulders and upward."

Even in the most abstruse questions, he never abandons this simplicity, so hard to achieve; he would rather teach than appear learned.

We have already spoken of his objectivity and its cause, but we must refer to it again here, insofar as it is a mark of his genius, unsurpassed in the genius of others. While we admire the good-naturedness of Socrates, and the nobility of Plato and Aristotle, we are bound to admit that, from the point of view of philosophy and helpfulness to others, it is better to be above these exquisite human characteristics, in the realms of pure thought. Stylishness has really nothing to do with truth, and the philosopher needs clearness of vision more than polished manners.

It is only the greatest personality that can be impersonal; can forget his status and personal greatness and discuss a question entirely on its merits.

This objectivity, and his constructive mind, led him to uphold certain views that, in his philosophical surroundings, were in danger of being repudiated. He was able to defend his position against the Platonic idealism that held the day. He insisted on the substantial character of the world, its real causality, and the validity of its actions and interactions. He upheld the autonomy of thought against the false mystics of his day, and the validity of experience against those who believed in innate ideas, and the *a priori* proofs of the existence of God. Amid strong opposition, he upheld the unity of man, the unity of soul and body, and thus prepared the way for the modern theories of psychophysiology.

It was to Aristotle that he was chiefly indebted for these principles, but he developed them on broader lines. He realized their full force and import and grasped the link that connects them with objective truth, as opposed to false idealism. "Aristotle," he says, "does not seek truth in the same way as other philosophers." (He is thinking especially of Plato.) "He begins with sensible, observable things and proceeds to things separated from matter . . . They, on the other hand, set out to apply intelligible and abstract things to things of sense."[25]

The height to which his thought aspired necessitated a firm hold on reality; the tall tree must be deep-rooted. He built on a

[25] In III *Metaphysics*, lect. 1.

solid foundation, so unlike the airy construction of the Sophists. He was in contact with things, not merely with ideas. And he was in touch with other thinkers and respectful toward tradition. Hence, by a comparison of the views of great men, he was able to control his own speculations. Knowledge is, after all, only a mode of living and therefore depends upon life and upon living beings. Cut it off from these, and it becomes a prey to chimeras. When, however, it is necessary to choose from what they offer, men and epochs must be prudently distinguished, without any violent reaction or rupture. "His mind," wrote Doctor Willmann, "was like a lake which receives the torrents of water from every side, and allows the impurities that they contain to sink to the bottom, so as to remain a clear reflector of the blue sky above."

St. Thomas's genius had just the right proportions of moderation and boldness. While it is true that a genius that is somewhat unbalanced does more for the progress of thought than a second-rate mind, the really marvelous genius is the one that is well balanced and whose daring takes the form of raising commonplaces to sublime ideas.

Bossuet speaks of these unbalanced minds as "more able to push things to extremes than to prevent reason following its bias, and competent rather to collect ideas than to reduce them to their natural unity." If St. Thomas does not allow his reason to follow its natural bias in this way, it is not because he is timid, but because he is extremely daring.

Conditions being what they were in his age, his prudence, docility, humility, and piety could not prevent his being a revolutionary. It sounds strange to call one a revolutionary whose sole intention was to restore order, but really order is the end, although not always the outcome, of every revolution. It was his love of truth and his clearsightedness that made him speak a new language and seem subversive. He marches straight ahead, and his free step is bolder than deeds of valor, as his humility is more exalted than pride. He is never surprised. We may wander around him, looking in vain for the reconciliation of truths. Then he will speak to us in a strange tongue, but strange only because it is eternal.

We must repeat, however well known it may be, that the most outstanding characteristic of his genius was his power of synthesis. He had the knack of getting at the roots of things and following up all their ramifications. His special aptitude was to centralize, unify, and disentangle, and thus to render things clear.

A principle is the germ of expansion, and nobody knew better than he did how to foster the germ and bring it to maturity. While he cannot be said to have *invented* the guiding principles of science, still, it was he who brought them into play, and surely he who could discover their full force, and could properly use and apply them, may be called their inventor. Capable of dealing with a multitude of facts, ideas, texts, and documents, sacred and profane, he was able to make from them a synthesis, simple and grand without wrong emphasis or false perspective.

In his system, the solution of the smallest practical question involves the whole universe; its whole framework is apparent in its least application. In Michelangelo's figures, noble and elegant as they are, we can always see the skeleton. Beethoven works out a symphony by subtle variations of the theme, but the theme is always there. In Shakespeare or in Corneille, the lively trait, the unexpected answer, or the sudden gesture are meant only to bring out the soul of a person or of a situation. Similarly, the far-reaching principles in St. Thomas, the skeleton of his system, his whole mind and broad outlook are revealed in every development and every particular conclusion. Everything flows from first principles. Nothing is a mere expedient. This sense of unity, this sense of the correlation of all ideas and of all beings is one of the most striking characteristics of his writings. He sets his course by the stars.

"Philosophy," wrote Novalis, "is a kind of homesickness, a longing to be at home everywhere. St. Thomas's ambition was to be thus present by his thought in every part of the universe. He never for a moment relinquished it. He found science, as it were, a heap of iron filings, and he turned it into a perfect system, governed by definite laws. He united things without confusing them. He could gauge the relative values of the great and the small, and classify each according to its proper laws. He found the absolute in every particular value, and *vice versa.* He set out to discover in God the origin of everything in the world. He fulfilled Amiel's description of a great mind as an *Esprit sphérique, qui voit tout, sait tout, envellope tout.*[26]

It is true that there was more than one error into which his synthesis might have led him. There are philosophers who build up their system with abstract concepts, the value of which is purely logical, and thus turn living nature into a piece of machinery. The poet, on the other hand, makes everything live, but blurs the outlines and the mutual relations of things. Between these extremes is the eclectic, who makes a clever selection, but who never gets to the heart of nature, where is to be found the unity of all his theses. The true philosopher must unite all things by probing them more deeply. There is no other way of reconciling facts,

[26]"A comprehensive mind, which sees all, knows all, and embraces all."

doctrines, tendencies, or men. St. Thomas had not that "way of keeping assiduously on the surface of things." He goes straight to the truth, where all things are reconciled; to reality, to being, where, divine and human, every partial truth, every correct tendency, and every age finds its justification.

He dwelt in a region between concrete reality and its principles, and could therefore discover the relationship of the one with the other, deducing facts from principles, or principles from facts, according as he possessed the one or the other at the outset. This is not, as has been asserted, "weighing reality in shadowy scales." While it is possible to be too abstract (and we may grant that this was true, in a sense, of St. Thomas), reality is not thereby lost sight of, because the abstract is the measure of reality; indeed the abstract is just as real, since it is the operation of a real being, the intelligence. The platinum bar that represents the standard meter is itself a material thing, but, at a certain temperature, it is a true measure of material things.

St. Thomas is moreover just as clever in matters of detail as he is in tracing the bold outlines; his breadth of outlook in no way impairs his analysis of particular points. He analyzed only where it was necessary to test an element in his great system and he avoided subtlety that served no purpose. It was not his wish to astonish by microscopic analysis; he preferred to convince by clear vision, aware that the vast expanse of truth surrounds, like an aureole, each minute element.

Let us finish with some account of his moral and mystical genius, as this will help us to form a better idea of his genius in metaphysics. It has been said that, in metaphysics, St. Thomas is "superficial." That was not the opinion of Leibnitz. Such a view shows either a complete absence of knowledge or an uncommon lack of judgment.

On first reading, we may be misled by his deliberate inaccuracies and by his provisos, which are full of meaning for the learned, easy for the beginner, and clear to all. These were due to the depth and breadth of his thought, to his clarity, and to the didactic character of his writings. He had a happy knack of avoiding an explanation that was inopportune, of economizing the truth, and of shelving by a noncommittal answer a difficulty that he did not wish to discuss. This should be a matter for praise rather than blame; we should admire his silence, as we admire the pauses in a magic symphony.

The principal attacks on Thomistic metaphysics come from those whose own philosophy is either physical or idealistic, the two extremes that reduce metaphysics to a branch of physics and psychology respectively.

St. Thomas, on the contrary, is a real metaphysician. He places the object of this science in *Being*, taken in its widest sense, and in the common attributes of being; he seeks an explanation of derived being, not in itself, but in the profounder principles of its source. He reiterates Aristotle's saying that we can no more build up the world of experience with experience than we can build houses with houses. The whole object of metaphysics is to try to grasp the mystery that lies behind visible things.

It is only a great mind that can move in this higher sphere of the eternal principles that govern our changeable, temporal world. Many are ignorant of its very existence, unless they know of it through their religion. Still, all thought presupposes it, and the task of a genius in metaphysics is to unravel its mysteries and make it known to others to express the deepest of nature's secrets and speak nature's most exalted language.

St. Thomas was primarily a theologian, and his metaphysics were chiefly built up around the mysteries of God. Not that this prevented him from using his great gifts to form a complete metaphysical system. He was naturally led to this from the fact that God, who is self-subsisting Being, in one sense coincides with the object of metaphysics, just as the sun coincides with the real image of it, which the astronomer sees in his telescope. He therefore made every effort to probe the mystery of God in philosophy, and as far as possible to explore his intimate truths. Not even the supreme mystery of the Trinity was beyond his speculations. He skirted around it and argued about it from outside, rather as a skilled mathematician invents *formulae* for unknown realities. God was impenetrable, but he could circle around him, and light up the frontiers; and in the penumbra, the God-fearing soul finds peace.

In treating of creation, he strives to explain the inner workings of *being*, before it becomes a *phenomenon*, the conditions that make it a phenomenon, and the nature of a phenomenon, which is also a form of being, since appearance has a reality of its own and needs explaining just as much as any other reality. Yet his teaching is not esoteric; it exactly reflects reality.

A genius in metaphysics, he is possibly an even greater genius in moral theology. His very sanctity made it inevitable. Abounding charity urges the philosopher to mix with men, as Raphael walked with the young Tobias, and showed him how to overcome the monstrous fish and to find the medicines that he sought. St. Thomas thought in order to serve others, and his thought is colored by this solicitude.

Scholasticism has been accused of atrophying the mind, and drying up the emotions. If that be so, then, as Auguste Comte says of positivism, these effects are produced only in its *organes vulgaires*. It is certainly not true of St. Thomas.

But something more is required besides the inclination to serve. There must be a certain aptitude for morals, and this could not be lacking in one who was remarkable for his sound judgment, discrimination, accuracy, and good sense. If "most prudent" was one of the titles given to St. Thomas by his friends, is it not prudence, in fact, that is the essential virtue in moral principles as it is in practical morals? The common belief that the faculty of abstraction is opposed to common sense is a gross error. It might be true of those whose outlook is not wide enough to envisage both, but a genius is bound to realize the metaphysical foundation of morals, and the necessary and eternal principles that govern our contingent acts. "An incomplete theory," writes Novalis, "is ruinous to practical affairs, but a complete theory safeguards them." If we grant, with Goethe, that "different philosophies are merely different forms of life," we are bound to admit that a great philosopher must be a great moral legislator as well. It is because the vulture soars so high that it catches its prey upon the plains.

St. Thomas's moral theology has all the characteristics of his metaphysics. The main theses are accurately defined, while there is an extraordinary wealth of detail. We have only to read his treatise on the passions in the *Prima Secundae*, or his account of the secondary virtues in the *Secunda Secundae*, to see how subtle he can be.

Yet, to cope with the contingencies of everyday life, his moral genius had to be extremely adaptable, broadening out to the wide possibilities of real life and narrowing down to the principles of morality proper. A morality as exact as geometry is necessarily deceptive; it is a sort of cubism, in which the living figures are unrecognizable. Moreover, he is very different from certain casuists. He considered it a contradiction to speak of really concrete cases of conscience as solvable in the abstract, without reference to the subject and circumstances of the particular actions. It is impossible, he maintains, to define the individual by a string of notions, and every moral case is essentially individual, and therefore "ineffable." This does not deny the possibility of definite decisions in moral matters; it simply maintains that this science has limitations and that facts and conscience are beyond its scope.

St. Thomas had a genius for moderating these cases, as well as a genius for definite decisions. He united the Greek aptitude for defining and the Roman respect for law. His treatment of justice and laws, and his *De Educatione Principum* show him at once politician, lawmaker, and legal adviser — in short, the complete moralist. For politics, despite the modern interpretations of the word, is only a development, and an application to collective facts of the aims of individual men, and of the principles of the moral law. It is not a branch of physics, unconnected with the higher ends of human life.

Lastly, St. Thomas is a genius in his treatment of the mystic life, because mysticism bears the same relation to metaphysics and to morality, in the higher order of things, as these sciences bear to law, sociology, and politics, in our ordinary life. Mysticism deals with what is divine in us, in the same way that metaphysics deals with abstract thought, and moral theology with our natural acts. Emerson's description of Plato as the "Euclid of Sanctity" could be even more aptly applied to St. Thomas. Better than Plato, he formulated, as far as is possible, mysteries that, although not in themselves capable of formulation, may be defined extrinsically, explained by analogy, enunciated provisionally, and be shown to follow definite laws. He expounds clearly what the greatest mystics have sometimes confused in a cloud of imagery. He treats of ecstasies and deep love in an intellectual, not emotional, way.

Yet his knowledge of the inner life of the soul was not merely theoretical; he lived the life and experienced the ecstasies, but always with his emotions under control. He was to see in an ecstasy these limitations of his work, and to cry out, when the sublimity of divine truth overpowered him, "Here must my writings cease."

It is extraordinary how, as he rose higher in the supernatural, he seemed, as Barrès says of Dante, to be nearer to nature. He was driven to insist and to depend more and more upon the analogical character of the relations between creature and Creator. Yet his words are always exact, and, whether his principles are taken from Scripture or from reason, his proofs are always rigorous and rational.

His holiness was intellectual, and he gave intellectual expression to the deep, mystical experiences of the greatest souls. His inner, mystical life, his secret communing with God, become in his writings so many abstract concepts, to all appearances as lifeless as the principles of geometry. He does not use the language of a St. Teresa or a Ruysbroek or a John of the Cross. His vocation was to be a constraining and sobering influence; everything was subordinated to his proper work of teaching, which was not allowed to suffer for the sake of discussing what had no direct bearing on his teaching. The heart and the imagination must be rigorously subjected to the intelligence. His asceticism, his religion, his holiness, his oblation, adoration, holocaust was the right use of his reason. "The hero," says Emerson, "is he who is steadfastly concentrated," and it is in this sense that St. Thomas was a genius in philosophy, morality, and mysticism.

Chapter Six

St. Thomas's Teaching

In order to discover the genius of St. Thomas at work in his teaching, it would be necessary to analyze the numerous works in which that teaching is contained; it would be necessary to give a more or less detailed and critical summary of it. That we have attempted elsewhere, for those interested in philosophy.[27] We must, however, give a brief review of it, if only to show that, although he borrowed largely from others, and was supremely impersonal, St. Thomas's doctrine was the achievement of his own original genius.

Pierre Duhem once remarked that he found in St. Thomas not so much a synthesis as a mosaic, and a "desire of synthesis." To the real student of St. Thomas, this statement appears most unjust. The one thing that continually strikes him is his unity of plan, which is felt even when least looked for, like the unity of line and mass in a cathedral.

It is true that St. Thomas borrowed a great deal, but the whole value, the very meaning of what he borrowed is due to its being

[27] Cf. A. G. Sertillanges, *Foundation of Thomistic Philosophy*, trans. G. Anstruther, O.P. (London: Sands and Co., 1931).

inserted in the unifying plan that he constructed. If he had borrowed everything in this way, it would not have lessened the philosophical value of his work. "Every master finds his materials ready at hand," says Barrès. "Thought," says Emerson, "is the property of him who can entertain it; and of him who can adequately place it."[28] The philosopher receives a thought from another, and his task consists in finding out exactly how it fits into his philosophy. He adopts it precisely because it holds this place.

Every really great man is a creator, but it does not follow that he must create an alphabet; he uses the existing one for coining new words. Just as it is not the letters that create new words, so it is not thoughts that create new philosophies, but the ordering and subordinating of them, the interplay of elements in a carefully planned framework, which connects them all with their first causes.

Hence, it is not the details and particular theories that are of importance in a great philosophy, but the breath of intellect that vivifies them, the web that binds them together, the vague, primary intuition, and the final, complete synthesis which give life to the whole.

According to St. Thomas, intellects, angelic and human, are gradated by the fewness of the principles by which a whole series of truths are known. His own intellectual greatness depended upon the fact that he was able to range an infinity of conclusions under comparatively few principles. This, far from being a "mosaic," is a real work of art, a living, organic construction.

Every thinker makes use of pre-existing theories; his special work is to use his own thought to put them in their due place. Henceforth, he works alone; he uses his own judgment. What he

[28] Emerson, *Representative Men*, "Shakespeare."

rejects is scarcely less important than what he chooses, and both are absorbed into his final achievement. It may happen that what was negligible before is now of sovereign value.

It has been wittily said, "It is not enough to plunder one's predecessors; they must be assassinated." St. Thomas never "assassinates" in this way, but how much he overshadows many of those whom he has been blamed for plagiarizing! Even St. Augustine, great as he is, hardly holds now the position he held before St. Thomas's time. And we have already seen that, according to Emile Boutroux, "The most important work of Aristotle was the Christian philosophy," by which is meant Thomism.

Having answered that criticism — which, I believe, is in some quarters a most unphilosophical attempt to blacken his name — we must sketch the general trend of St. Thomas's philosophy without attempting to give even an approximate outline of it.

A glance at the index to the *Summa Theologica* will show that everything, not only his theology, but his philosophy too, is centered in God. Spinoza's philosophy has a similar orientation, and so must every complete system of doctrine, for in God is to be found the ultimate explanation of the whole of knowledge. All our ideas begin and end with God. All explanation is by universal principles, and ultimately by the First Principle. He who does not see as far as God is shortsighted, however far he may see, and he who does not view things from as far away as God is too near to see them fully. To refer things to God is the only way to put them in true perspective and thereby to understand them aright. We cannot determine the essence, limits, or proportions of anything without this reference to the Supreme Being.

A still more fundamental reason for this procedure was that *Being* is basically one, and is one in God. This bears out the great principle that, in philosophy, doctrine and method coincide.

Nowadays there is a good deal of ridicule about this *Philosophy of Being*, despite its support by the greatest thinkers of all ages. *Being* has been called "that meaningless and mysterious verbalism" which would have achieved success "in a world devoid of reality."[29] Evidently, no world is so empty as the conceptual world of one who denies it reality, but then, as a consequence, any reality there might be remains unaffected by such a conception. Taken in its most universal sense, *being* is more real than any of its multifarious participations; to deny this is at once a form of atheism and a warping of the highest faculties of the intelligence.

The main problem of philosophy was exactly the same for St. Thomas as it had been for Plato — namely, how the multiple comes from the one, and how it can be reunited to it. Identity and variety, differentiation and reintegration, emanation and return were the main discussions of Plato, of the Alexandrine Neo-Platonists, and of St. Thomas, although, of course, with important differences.

Whether we consider all things as essence and existence, substance and accident, thought and object, spirit and matter, knowledge and will, they always necessarily connote a relationship with something relatively *one*. Here the multiple, although real, is secondary and derived, and consequently reducible. The formulation and solution of the problem of the universe involves the setting out of all these in their true relations with the *one*.

Everything that the mind understands witnesses to a certain homogeneity, which enables things to be synthesized. The intelligence is not content with stray straws; it must have the sheaf. The mind is the natural judge of being; it equals it in extension, and its living, passive operation represents the active evolution of being.

[29] Cf. Paul Valéry, Preface au Léonard de Vinci.

Now, what is this power that can connect things in the real order, as the mind connects them in the ideal, in order to understand them? What is the bond that binds this universal sheaf? What is the source that all things presuppose? What is the absolute, homogeneous term that will explain the relative homogeneity of things? For the latter cannot be first, since, being relative and having differences, it implies a participation in some common, anterior thing, and a divergence from it.

The answer to this essential question is God. We approach God by apparently very different ways, but they all fundamentally come to this: the ulterior implies an anterior, diversity implies homogeneity, the multiple implies a unity.

Whether we follow everyday experience, scientific empiricism, common sense, or genius, we are led to the same conclusion. It is sufficient to notice that the objects of our knowledge present a certain order; there are categories, degrees, causes and effects, antecedents and consequences, means and ends. In short, the universe, in every sense of the word, and considered in all its possible relations, is seen to be what Kant calls an immense *conditioning*. From whatever phenomenon we start, we rise from one condition to another, whether real or ideal, until, at the top — for there must be a top, otherwise all these conditions are meaningless — we reach the Unconditioned, God, who is self-sufficient, the center of all expansion, the first Being and source of all things.

This, of course, brings us face-to-face with a mystery, a mystery that is the only adequate explanation of all things. We can name it and qualify it only by its effects; but it still remains the highest form of our knowledge, as well as that about which we know least. Silence is here the highest form of adoration.

Once we have reached this point, we descend again, by the synthetic method, and thereby explain the relations of things with God. Just as we began with things to rise to God, so we start back from God to reach things. St. Thomas uses the latter method in theology (where God's existence is granted) and the former in his philosophy. As a matter of fact, both methods are used in conjunction in all his works, although they are always clearly defined.

But everywhere is apparent this central focus of thought, whence the mind determines the relations of reality by deriving it from God and is led back to God from every point where these relations touch things. It is this that gives to his expositions, when slightly amplified, their sense of completeness, and makes his system revolve with the perfection of the solar system.

God is the first Being, the perfect, full Being, who is "virtually all things," since all things have their rise and *raison d'être* in him. He is the All — so much so that what comes from him "is not an addition to him." "In him we live and move and have our being." Scotus Erigena went so far as to say that, in a sense, God created himself by giving being to his creatures — an exaggeration that brings out how God possesses all being, to what extent creatures are united to him and to one another, and how all things are homogeneous, fundamentally identical, reducible to a common principle, and all converging, because all are divine.

God is assembled being; the world is distributed being. The object of Thomistic philosophy is to classify this distribution, and to reassemble, by an alternate systole and diastole.

Nearest to God we find pure spirit; next comes man, who is spirit joined to matter, and below him the instinctive, living organism of the brute. Then comes vegetal life, then beings and activities differentiated by forms and specific properties, and lastly, pure matter, the common substratum of everything that evolves or changes.

These are all participations in the divine being, concrete resemblances of the Prototype, a gradated descent of the All-Being, who loses nothing of his transcendence by being thus participated in. And these things differ only by the degree in which they participate in God, by the way in which they (imperfectly) reflect their first Principle, by their relation to God's being, whence is derived all in his creation that has number, weight, measure, mode, species, or order.

Spirit and matter, in particular, differ only as the greater and lesser, perfect and imperfect, actual and potential. The act of knowing and the thing actually known are identical, and where the act is perfect, the two are perfectly identified in God. Spinoza's idea that the infinite Substance is manifested both in thought and in extension vitiates both his pantheism and his dualism. That which is manifested is not a simple *mode:* it subsists, and the connection between the extended body and the thought is due to a more ultimate actualization.

This equally answers the dualism of Descartes and disposes of his problem of the union of soul and body. Man is not a mixture of two heterogeneous and irreducible substances; he is a degree. It is true that we speak of him as composite, but that is due to our analysis of him; in reality, there is neither body nor soul, but simply man, just as water, before analysis, is not oxygen and hydrogen, but simply water.

Man is not a spirit enclosed in matter, an "imprisoned angel," a "fallen god," or a monster; he is an autonomous being, and what multiplicity there is in him is due to the imperfection of his being, for the further a being is removed from God, the more multiple it becomes in extension, time, and movement.

The famous dispute over the unity of the substantial form in man, on which St. Thomas laid such stress, and which is still an open question, brings out this point clearly. It involves the whole of his metaphysics. He never wavered, although as fully alive as anyone to the difficulties that his theory created. If man is one, how can we explain his twofold origin, from God and from his parents? If man is one, how can we conceive that the soul is immortal, when the body corrupts? Thus, while the problems of individuation and of survival might remain dubious, the general trend of his metaphysics commanded assent and furnished solutions to the objections of materialism on the one hand, and an equally one-sided "angelism" on the other.

Now let us see what follows from these principles.

God comes first. The world proceeds from God, without, however, being separated from him. This divine parentage which binds all things to their common principle, creates in them a tendency toward it. This accounts for their activity and determines their end. Every being thus tends spontaneously toward its principle, and the truer the principle, the more powerful the tendency. A true principle is one that governs, not only the inner reality of what proceeds from it, but also the development and destiny of that reality. The infant seeks his mother for food, the student his master for knowledge; the soldier obeys his officer in the hope of victory. Similarly, all things tend to God for their being, for perfection of every kind, for their *good*. Created being seeks God, because it will more fully realize itself by a fuller participation in God. It finds its true form and realizes its end, perfection, by making itself more like to God.

Nowadays, these ideas of finality are rejected by scientists, although science has really no power to deal with a question like this, which is metaphysical. And is it really more illuminating and rational to represent the world as a sort of monstrous machine, driven by some quite indefinable power, than to represent it as an immense desire, giving rise to an immense effort? Still, the two aspects are not exclusive but only complementary.

Anyhow, St. Thomas held that *being* emanated from God, and strove to be reunited to him; that this desire actuates reality and accounts for the ceaseless travail of all creation.

Each being tends toward God according to its own nature. All travel by the same route, but all do not go equally far. Just as nature is a hierarchy, so are its laws and, consequently, its ends. The material world is created, follows its allotted curve, and corrupts: the plant buds, grows, gives its fruit, and dies; the brute has a more varied destiny, but radically the same as the plant's. But to the spirit's journey there is no end; in its rich unfolding, in its mighty quest, it can reach even to God himself. It has the power of thinking all *being,* of penetrating to the cause of being, and it is destined, by nature and by grace, to be united to that cause. Man will not be confused with God, for by this union he more fully realizes his own being; but he will be joined to God and, in a sense, will be deified. His destiny might almost be called a Christian Nirvana.

St. Thomas held that the material universe was permanent and would return to the *perfect* under some form that it is impossible to foretell. The *new heavens* and *new earth* were not empty words to him. It is true that he was influenced by the then-prevailing cosmology, but his thought is sufficiently independent of it to be adapted to modern theories. But when all is said and done, cosmology, ancient or modern, will always be faced by a mystery.

But to return to the particular case of man, which interests us the most: we must classify the various ways in which we tend toward God, according to the different elements of our being. As material, vegetal, and sensitive beings, we would have no special destiny if these faculties were autonomous; but they are not. Since our being is one, all its parts are subordinated to and directed toward their common end, which is the perfection of the whole being. Our material faculties are ordained to serve our life; our material life, our sensitive life; sensitive life, thought; natural thought, faith; and faith, the eternal vision of God.

Hence, the intelligence is the principal factor in this return to God, although it is the will that creates the desire, just as in lower beings, while their form is their essential part, there is a certain tendency to which is due their self-development and the realization of their end. It is this fact that gives knowledge its sovereign value in the natural order, and faith in the supernatural.

St. Thomas, following Aristotle, makes knowledge, in the widest sense of the word, the highest, natural, human perfection. "Happiness is the joy produced by truth."[30] The study of wisdom is more perfect and sublime, more useful and delightful, than any other pursuit of mankind."[31] "The ultimate end of all things is the good of the intellect, which is truth."[32] But wisdom can have a much wider meaning than as understood by Aristotle. In the learned, faith completes natural knowledge; in the ignorant, it takes the place of knowledge, while, provided we do not misuse our freedom, it will be revealed in all its fullness in the Beatific Vision.

Thus, knowledge leads us through things back to God, and faith melts before the vision of God. The other parts of our nature

[30] *Summa Theologica*, II-II, Q. 3, art. 4 (quoting St. Augustine).

[31] *Contra Gentiles*, I, ch. 2.

[32] Ibid., ch. 1.

attain their perfection in the new surroundings, to which they, too, are destined. The doctrine of the resurrection of the body is thus seen to fill a great need, which is acutely felt in philosophies divorced from the Faith.

This aspect, however, seemed to St. Thomas of secondary importance. It was a consequence of the vision, a communication to the body of a higher vitality, the result of its union with God. What chiefly impressed him was the marvelous expanse of knowledge that this vision opened out. For, although the principal object of the vision is God, it necessarily includes everything else.

He was greatly attached to the theory that, in order to know anything, we must have within us, in an ideal way, the being that we know. Aristotle holds that the soul is, in a sense, all things, because it is capable of knowing all things. Hence, a single being is capable of possessing in itself all the perfection of the world. It is easy to understand why the ancient philosophers considered this reflection of the world as the soul's greatest perfection. We go further and find this same perfection in the vision of God. As St. Gregory says, "What shall they not see, who see him, who sees all things?"[33]

It remains to state the conditions for enjoying this vision, which, with God's grace, we have to work for ourselves. This brings us to morality and the broad principles of ethics, which are governed by the same uniform laws. The highest of human activities is contemplation, because it is the nearest approach to man's end, which is intellectual. By contemplation is meant, not only what the word signifies in mysticism, but knowledge of any kind, and art, insofar as it is intellectual.

[33] Quoted by St. Thomas, *Quaest. De Veritate*, Q. 2, art. 2.

Knowledge, in its widest sense, begins with the knowledge of nature; this leads to philosophy in general, which, in turn, leads to metaphysics. To know and to "rationalize" matter cannot be an end in itself, since matter contains in itself neither its *raison d'être*, nor its end.

We must bear in mind that this order is an ideal, which is only ultimately to be realized. Here on earth, this very ultimate realization often necessitates a reversal of the process. Practice follows upon theory, and contemplation is allowed to be determined by action.

Further, as matter is, in a certain sense, spirit, so action is, in a certain sense, thought. It is a kind of alloy both of the thought that is revealed and of the thought that is searched for — the former, because every action is the outcome of a thought; the latter, because every realization is a return from, and an amplification of, thought. Every realization creates some kind of leisure, and thereby makes contemplation possible; if it is morally good, it is as meritorious as the contemplation that it makes possible. When we attain our end, action as we now understand it will give place to a higher form of activity. Our final end will be "the most noble use of man's noblest faculty, for the highest object."

It may be argued that in this great theory, the distinction between natural and supernatural creates an irreconcilable dualism, thereby marring the unity that God obviously intended should characterize his creation. The argument is worthless. Natural and supernatural are distinctions that apply only to creatures — that is, to beings that are dependent and gradated. In God, there is neither natural nor supernatural, but simply God. We distinguish, because we participate in God and communicate with him in two different degrees, as in a binary rhythm, and we analyze these two degrees, without ever implying that they are really distinct.

Our nature has been created, as it were, double, because of the double end to which we are destined; the higher, or super, nature tends to the higher end, which is our last end, pure and simple. Therefore, the unity of the whole reality is not destroyed. The supernatural does not create in us an ontological and final duality, anymore than does rationality in attaching itself to our sensitive life, or the sensitive to the vegetal, or the vegetal to the physicochemical activity of the tissues. These are all continuous, make up one integral existence, and normally produce the same results.

A further argument may be drawn from the fact that God chose the Incarnation as the means of realizing these supernatural ends. The whole order of grace centers on our Lord, who is God and Man, the common Brother, the Head of the entire creation, and the point of contact between Creator and creature.

In a very true sense, everything comes from the One, everything is one, tends toward the One, and is consummated in the One. There is a simple, perfect unity underlying the enormous diversity of forms.

We have dwelt mostly upon man in our survey, because knowledge is, after all, made for man. But we must not fail to notice the stupendous effort that St. Thomas makes to integrate his philosophy and theology by an account of the pure spirit. This treatise on the angels is one of his greatest achievements.

The angels seem to have awakened in him a very special curiosity and devotion. In the beginning of his *Opusculum De Creaturis Spiritualibus*, he says pleasantly, "Not being able to do the work of the angels in choir, we can at least write about them." He made a point of sifting the opinions of ancient philosophers concerning spirits, and this is an additional proof that his rigid method did not dry up the religious fervor latent in his writings.

His treatise on the angels is a remarkable work. It is like a complicated mathematical treatise, with a few passages from Scripture here and there, but primarily derived from rational psychology, and natural theology, the two great sciences that it links together. Although our interests today are in other directions, we ought not to neglect this monumental work.

∞

This meager outline should be enough to show the genius of St. Thomas's undertaking, its masterly fulfillment, and, above all, his sureness in the midst of dangers on every point of doctrine.

He assimilated not only the principles of Aristotle, but also Platonism, Alexandrine Neo-Platonism, and the Platonism of Augustine, the Pseudo-Denis, and the *Liber de Causis*. He found a place even for Parmenides, with his theory of the unity of being. But he has restated the doctrines of all these authors, as well as the particular theses that follow from their principles.

St. Thomas held that, while *being* was one, it was virtually multiple, in which he differed from Parmenides. He held with Plato that God was perfectly free to manifest himself in creation or not, in which he differed from Aristotle and the Alexandrine school. He held with Plotinus that *being* emanates from God and returns to him, but he differed in that he substituted for Plotinus's vague and mystic explanations a complete hierarchy of values, drawn from experience, which distinguishes species and being, and includes even the dogmas of faith.

His doctrine is monistic, but without the errors of monism, dynamistic, but without the errors of dynamism, which denies substances and makes everything the action of forces. It is intellectualistic, because it identifies being and thought, but it is voluntarist as well, because it makes thought engender love, as *being* engenders force. Thought directs our love to God, and love, our thoughts. Everything is done by love and for love, and love is the consummation of all things.

Lastly, his doctrine is at once creationist and evolutionist. It is creationist insofar as it makes everything come freely from God, and thus depend upon *being*, and not upon some indefinable chaos. It is evolutionist insofar as it makes everything return to God. Medieval physics made it necessary for St. Thomas to hold that this return was an unchanging cycle, but there is nothing to prevent the modern Thomist from adopting the modern theory of evolution, and maintaining that things develop in a straight line, whose last term is unknown to us.

This enables us to avoid the exaggerations and fallacies of isolated theories, which lead to manifest impossibilities. This St. Thomas believed was the only possible way to establish an order out of the multifarious, and apparently opposed, notions that we get from things. There seemed no other solution to the problem of the world, as our entire experience presents it, and in its main outlines, his system is seen to be perfectly complete.

It is sometimes objected that the reduction of the multiple to the one, which is its goal, is not de facto realized, because the multiple is not eventually destroyed, and the multiple and the one must both subsist. The answer is that, if the multiple so returns to the one that nothing now remains but a divine existence, and all is as it was before the cycle began, then there is surely no purpose achieved by creation. Or are we expected to turn the entire creation into some sort of pointless symphonic movement?

The multiple must subsist, but only as subordinated to the one, explained and bound together by the one, to such a degree that it is virtually contained in the one, with no part of it free and independent.

In this doctrine, to quote Lachelier, "all things harmonize, and nothing is confused." That is what makes it a perfect system without for a moment denying that there is a mystery behind it, which can be ever further explored. St. Thomas never claimed to have spoken the last word; he intended to be true as far as he went, and to offer a complete system in outline. It is independent of any new data of cosmology, physics, or positive psychology, because he treats of it metaphysically. He had no fears of ever being out of date, because he based it on the best-established phenomena, although he illustrates his teaching by examples taken from the physical theories of his time, which are now rejected. His sole object was to take up a true position with regard to reality and to make a general framework. He did not aim at completeness of detail.

He respected the mystery; this *terra incognita* was marked on his map, and he did his best to describe it from without, but always with fine scientific caution. He did not even attempt a scientific proof of Providence. Cajetan rightly praises him for this; scientific caution of this sort in a theologian cannot but increase our confidence in him.

He realized, and often says, that the human mind must needs, in this world, move between two zones of darkness: matter below and mystery above. The latter is so intelligible that it dazzles us. We are forced to acknowledge, above and below, this unfathomable sea, and when, by the supreme effort of our reason, we try to sound it, we must not take the length of our line as any indication of its depth.

That is where St. Thomas shows his prudence; and genius allied to prudence is the essence of the truly wise man.

Chapter Seven

St. Thomas's Style

We must be careful not to dwell too long upon St. Thomas as a writer, for that would be to sin against brevity, and brevity is the chief characteristic of his style. He was unacquainted with that art of never having said enough, which many of our thinkers affect. His articles are short and compact, and the replies to objections even more so, but there is sublimity in his very silences.

Erasmus admired the Latin of the *Summa*, obviously not for its classical purity, but because of its high intellectual qualities, among which he certainly included this rich brevity, his *stylus brevis, grata facondia* — words that are found in the Office of his feast. It is the mark of a truly great mind to write with this nice discrimination, avoiding mere verbiage and giving only what is essential.

To those who are conversant with the problems that he discusses, St. Thomas is always clear precisely because of his power of seizing upon what is of primary importance and of leaving out secondary matters. His commentators will readily obscure his meaning, in explaining some point of their own; for true illumination, we must go to the master. Fortunately, we still have his works to explain what his commentators are driving at! It is quite a relief to return to him after cutting our way through their entanglements. Novalis rightly says, "The supreme, the purest, is also the commonest and the most comprehensible. The more a science becomes difficult and complicated, the more it is derived, impure, and mixed."

This brings us to another characteristic, closely akin to the first, if not identical with it — namely, his simplicity. By *simple* is meant a style that is not overcharged, complicated, or padded. St. Thomas's simplicity of style is as perfect as his freedom from complications and digressions. He shows his intellectual power without making a show of it, like a Hercules who makes no parade of his strength. He avoids our modern pedantry, our attitude of mystery, our way of throwing dust into people's eyes. His simplicity of style follows naturally from his simplicity of soul. All his phrases are the outcome of an ordered, sternly disciplined mind and exactly correspond to his ideas. He has no drapery; he sketches his ideas in the nude. He has no rhetoric, but, to use Claudel's phrase, "an almost literal expression of reality." His style is the style of a builder or engineer, who uses only primordial elements and basic means of assemblage.

This is all an effect of his objectivity. His style, like his thought, is objective, in that it is an exact replica of things. Each word represents a thing, each sentence a truth, each article a definite *ensemble*, each treatise a world. There is always an inherent order in his exposition. In drawing attention to the contents of the *Summa*, we saw that it revealed a complete system, and this is equally true of each article and of each proposition.

He writes direct from his mind, without recourse to the literary treasures that are the standby of most authors. He is hardly an "author," or even a "man," but rather a channel connecting us directly with intelligible truth.

We may with justice apply to him what Barrès says of Dante: "His grave, sculptural style is due to his immediate and composite vision of all spiritual truths."

There is a hidden connection between his style and the philosophy that he set out to expound. His contemporary St. Bonaventure was Augustinian and mystical and wrote in quite a different strain; similarly, St. Anselm and St. Bernard. Carpaccio, Paolo Ucello, and Michelangelo, on the one hand, and Titian, Veronese, Rubens, and Delacroix on the other, have a way of painting that corresponds to their different visions of the world. They all represent beauty, but the beauty of St. Thomas is severe. His definiteness and compactness grace his style, as the portraying of muscles enhances the beauty of a naked Doryphore or Apoxyomenos. It is impossible to modify it, shorten it, or add to it without spoiling the whole system. As a model of scientific exposition, it is scarcely paralleled in the best pages of Aristotle, or, in modern times, by Goethe or Claude Bernard.

Yet his writing cannot be called monotonous. When thought reigns alone, there is monotony, in the etymological sense of the word, if the *tonality* of the thought remains unaltered, and there is variety if the tonality alters. Each individual has his own skin, which changes as the individual grows, and that is the only variation to which it is susceptible. St. Thomas does not mind repeating himself when there is need; he uses the same expressions over and over again, when the same thought recurs, thus guiding the reader and pointing the road through difficult territory instead of confusing him by false synonyms and elegant variations.

We spoke of St. Thomas's sense of measure as one of the marks of his genius. It is equally evident in his literary form. He never pads; he never strains a point; he is never one-sided or unbalanced in his judgments. This again is the outcome of his philosophy, for he was dominated, not by the particular objects that he studied, but by their order and mutual dependence. Science is knowledge "by causes"; that is, it is concerned with the exact balance of coordinated series. Further, the essential of the entire creation is not this or that particular creature, but the cosmos.

He is just as impersonal in his exposition of truth as in his search for it. Without this character, he would not be objective, nor enjoy the same widespread influence. Impersonality is so bound up with truth that it impresses itself sooner or later on its followers. He who is far removed from himself and near to truth is, by that very fact, in contact with all intelligences.

Nevertheless, in reading him, we do have a sense of quiet power. Despite his dislike of ostentation, he cannot help impressing us. We feel that he is like a smoothly running machine, with all the power that its quiet implies. Here again is the art of the engineer. He substitutes for the playful humor of Plato, the grave serenity of Spinoza or Aristotle. It is an art free to follow its own deep longings. The free curve is the greatest achievement of geometrical precision.

The study of St. Thomas brings us peace; we derive confidence and joy from him, because we realize that all that he says proceeds from the love of truth, a love subject to God.

The epithet *dry* applied to his writings has no more meaning than when applied to Egyptian art, or to the metopes of the Parthenon or of the Throne of Venus at Thermes. A writer must be dry in that sense, if he is to say much in a few words and not put an obstacle between the mind and the truth.

We grant, however, that for a truly humanist presentation of thought, his style has its limitations, but these can be remedied by the cooperation of other thinkers and writers. The teacher need not be an orator; he may leave that to others. The organizer of ideas is not their popularizer. St. Thomas would have been the first to admit (indeed, he laid down the rules) that, besides the teaching by concepts and dogmatic propositions, there is the teaching by imagery, and the appeal to the emotions; to which are due the final triumph of truth in the world.

The builders of Memphis did not carve the colossal blocks destined for their temples. They measured them, cut them to size, and fitted them into place. It was left to those who came after to cut on them the story of their battles and royal hunts, and the images of their gods.

Chapter Eight

The Poetry of St. Thomas

In the previous chapter, we spoke of St. Thomas's scientific prose works. Here we may single out his religious poetry, which has carried his influence far beyond the narrow circle of thinkers for whom he seemed destined to write.

Remy de Gourmont's admiration for the Office of *Corpus Christi* is well known. But as early as the seventeenth century, Jean de Santeul, author of Latin poems of some merit, declared that he would willingly exchange all his works for one of St. Thomas's stanzas, as Gounod would have exchanged all his music for the chant of the *Preface*.

But we must first discuss whether St. Thomas considered that poetry had any doctrinal importance. M. Pierre Lasserre goes too far when he claims that in St. Thomas we have (as in Bossuet and Milton) "an epic rather than a philosophic type of intelligence." That seems to me only a half-truth. While it is true that there is something epic about the general trend of Thomism, it is nonetheless due to the philosophical character of St. Thomas. He creates, or re-creates, the ideas by the value that he communicates to them; he does not merely display them as in a panorama.

There is a real musical symmetry about the *Summa*, not because of some artifice in the distribution of its materials, but in its very structure; it is sprung like a Gothic cathedral, a lyric of pure thought.

In St. Thomas, doctrine has become harmonious after the manner of a symphony. It vibrates freely in all its parts and undulates from end to end, without any of those intermissions which falsify the key and break the harmony, without unresolved discords or any but expressive silences, by which I mean mysteries. Mysteries are not empty voids. They are more full of meaning than is anything else, and it is their very depth that makes them unfathomable. As such, they serve as links to ensure cohesion. Their purpose in a synthesis is to give unity and strength, and indeed, beauty to the whole.

In the brief sketch that we have given of this synthesis, one cannot fail to notice an underlying vein of poetry. To borrow Carlyle's phrase about Shakespeare, "all rounds itself off, into a kind of rhythmic coherence."[34]

St. Thomas sought the meaning of the whole visible world; what was its secret? His method is simplicity itself; he wrote down just what he saw, and his words are as clear as his vision. By this alone is he a poet, for a clear insight into the relations of all things is poetry in the deepest sense of the word, whether expressed in prose or verse.

Rhythm is the expression of the symmetry of time and space, a symmetry in the things themselves. Every poetic image is the expression of a relationship, and the deeper and truer the relationship, the more perfect the image. Looked at in this wise, the poet is an intuitive philosopher, and the philosopher a reflecting poet.

[34] Carlyle, *Heroes and Hero-Worship*, lect. 3.

All philosophy is an attempt to express the meaning and relations of things to God, whether of nature, human life, history, thought, or action, wherever they occur in the universe. It sets out to give a view of the whole of reality as seen from within, with the relations that give it its unity and its divine order. Anyone who succeeds in doing this with inspiration must be hailed at once as prophet and poet.

In these sublime regions, the difference of medium is unimportant. The philosopher uses concepts rather than images and rhythm; he explains the concrete in abstract language, whereas the poet uses the concrete to explain even the abstract. But always it is God and creation, man and the world, that are the rich pasture of both the poet and the philosopher. The former, by his emotions and imagination, is in contact with everything that is, while the latter strives successfully to be *Partout, dans l'univers, présent par sa pensée.*

We may quote the following fine passage of M. Pierre Lasserre, which seems to us an apposite description of the poetic appeal of St. Thomas's philosophy:

> The comparisons and images which he continually creates, with the ease and fertility of a great poet, furnish a thousand means of accommodating to his readers the visions of his faith and of his religious poetry — means adapted to the scholastic setting in which he mounts them. Hence his intellectual harmony, and his easy transition from one idea to another, which, even when he leads us to the most dizzy heights of abstraction, gives a charm to the *Contra Gentiles*.[35]

[35] *La Jeunesse d'Ernest Renan.*

Imagination and emotion in St. Thomas play a much larger part than is generally supposed.[36] We are too much taken up with the idea to notice the medium that conveys it, much less the secret resonance and the profound silences to which we have referred. A dry phrase becomes infused with poetry when written by an inspired genius.

But, although St. Thomas is a poet in his use of metaphor and simile, nevertheless his thought is not dependent upon his images, but precedes them: he is the poet of the abstract and makes imagery subservient.

Once only did he attempt poetry in the technical sense of the word. Was it because he thought, with Etienne Burnes, that "Poetry is the dove, destined to be sent on ahead when reason has reached its limit"? This does not seem to have been his motive. He was simply asked to write hymns on the Holy Eucharist, and he who had written so profoundly on this mystery in prose found it easy to obey. He believed that this was not a distraction, but another means of teaching the truth.

The Holy Eucharist embodies, in the highest possible way, the same Divine Word, which is the object of reason and faith, and which dwelt among us and became our daily bread. The love of truth, the love of Truth itself, the love of the ideas that are reflected in truth, the love of this sacrament were all one to him. He who linked together the various dogmas of faith sings the praises of him who unites all the members of the Church. As this sacrament is for all, so his hymns are for all, whereas his abstract writings, in themselves at least, are meant for a few.

[36] Few, for instance, would, without reflecting, dream of attributing to him an idea like the following, which nevertheless is quite authentic: "Hope, like smoke, from the fire of love, mounts up from life and vanishes in glory" (in *Epist. ad Ephes.* prologue).

Here St. Thomas found an outlet for his love of the Liturgy, instilled in him by the Benedictines, and for his emotions, to which his syllogistic method gave little scope.

Even in his hymns, he avoids singularities or individual lyricisms and mystic flights of fancy. He sings a song for the whole Church and voices the fervor that all should feel. Yet, in voicing fervor so deep, he loses nothing of his simplicity or facility of writing.

He uses the first person, but in the plural: "*nobis datus, nobis natus*"; his eagerness to carry us along with him is shown in his *Imperatives* (subjunctive in form) "*Praestet fides supplementum,*" "*Veneremur,*" "*Compar sit laudatio.*" His poetry is always joyous and triumphant, without any of the gloom of Jansenism or of the violent emotion of the fifteenth century. As is only fitting in one dedicated to the service of all, his poetry is concrete, the poetry of things, just as in Ecclesiastes and Proverbs. Again, by his use of stress and rhyme, he broke away from the ancient rules of prosody and came somewhere near the modern standard.

Both in argument and in form, then, his poetry is a simple extension of his didactic method. His lyrical form is one of ideas, not of burning words and ardent imaginings, although it is prompted by the same fervor of soul, which may be expressed and satisfied by either of these means.

He has no need to modify his method, or, as it were, change his state of soul, because his very philosophy had a poetic beauty, which was present to his mind when he turned to poetry. The beauty of his poems, like that of a diamond, is entirely the result of intense compression.

He differs from other great poets only superficially, for in all of them, it is the thought that makes the poem. In St. Thomas, the construction is more obvious, the song more reserved — characteristics which follow from that spiritual unity which, as we have said, was the basis of his teaching. His poetry is just as much bound up with his teaching as is his sanctity. Reason is always his guide, and the most rigorous exactitude is never sacrificed.

In reading his poetry, we are struck by its austerity, its terseness, and the avoidance of all unnecessary variety. It reads like a piece of music without accentuated pauses or unexpected marks of crescendo. It reminds one of Bach's first prelude, without the false *Ave Maria*, or his eighth, resounding through a cathedral.

The following is the stanza so admired by Santeul:

Se nascens dedit socium,
Convescens in edulium,
Se moriens in pretium,
Se regnans dat in praemium.[37]

In these four short lines, under a single rhyme, he treats of Christ's birth and life, of the Last Supper, of his redeeming death and his eternal triumph.

This is yet a further instance of his extraordinary balance of mind, and in circumstances in which we might have expected him to have relaxed the rigor of his method. The fact that he is as insistent here as ever on the strict rules of logic applied to his symbols and imagery shows that all his gifts are identified in their primary source and witnesses to his striking unity of soul.

[37] "By his birth he gave himself as our companion, at table as our food, at death as our ransom, and reigning he gives himself as our reward."

Chapter Nine

St. Thomas's Triumph

"The consequences of an undertaking are never fully foreseen," writes M. Abel Bonnard. St. Thomas, quietly tracing on the parchment his difficult characters, could he have foreseen the tremendous repercussions of his work, or the brilliance of his personal greatness, in a posterity that seems obliged periodically to revive or to give new impetus to his teaching?

The very sound of the name Thomas Aquinas concentrates in itself the sum-total of his fame. Like Plato, Aristotle, Shakespeare, Newton, and Pasteur, he has wholly absorbed admiration.

His destiny had been in some measure foreseen. We have already given the words of St. Albert the Great, prompted by the first, sudden blossoming of the genius of his young student. "He was the flower and glory of the world" was his final verdict when he who, more than any other, was developing Albert's thought, was snatched untimely from their common work.

Albert had himself shown the possibilities, and partially realized them, although unsystematically enough. He was as the wood that the fire has caught but not wholly kindled; some twigs or branches burning, but as yet no blaze. He, with many others, waited for the one pure flame, and he saw it rise. The result justified expectations, and people marveled at the work that welded into a single doctrine the materials and incomplete conclusions which were all that existed when he began.

Bartholomew of Lucca was the first to call him *Doctor Communis*, a title given at Paris to anyone of universal repute. Even in his lifetime, Alexander IV, Urban IV, and Clement IV had sanctioned his teaching, and he was practically their mouthpiece. When the news of his death arrived, the Faculty of Arts, which, in its philosophical capacity, was chiefly concerned in the new learning, was unstinted in its praise. In writing to his superiors, it proclaimed him "a morning star, or a new star in the heavens." They beg for his remains and undertake to raise an immortal monument to his memory.

Four years later, in 1278, the General Chapter held at Milan officially sanctioned his doctrine, which was henceforth to be a family treasure. It was the Church, however, that was to adopt, in ever greater degree, his intellectual armory. In 1318, addressing the delegates who came to petition for his canonization, Pope John XXII said, "This man has enlightened the Church more than all the other Doctors: one year spent on his works is more profitable than a lifetime devoted to other authors." This means that he contains the bond which unites what others have left scattered: and the bond is more important than the sheaf.

Pope after pope, right up to the present day, has constantly reiterated this praise. There was a time when the cult of scholasticism waned. Under the influence of the pagan Renaissance, and later of Cartesianism, and lastly of the Encyclopedists, the fame of Thomas was not loath to hide its head from the world, in anticipation of a revival. But in the Church there was no wavering. The Church never once let go of his discovered treasure: it was regarded as of paramount importance for the defense of religion. Leo XIII spoke of it as "The Church's protection and crown": "It belongs to the treasured possessions of humanity," as Barrès says, with less justice, of the *Divina Comedia*.

It may happen that renown of this kind defeats its own ends. Certain schools of thought, wishing, with this encouragement from the highest authorities, to be under his aegis, tried, by twisting St. Thomas's teaching, to justify their own unthomistic theories. But this is a penalty of greatness and serves to emphasize it.

In another, but happier, sense, St. Thomas has been swamped by his own glory. Because he is *Doctor Communis*, his teaching is for all; he appears not so much a man, as a gigantic column of granite supporting the globe. Or we may put it more simply. The *Summa Theologica* has become part of the very texture of the Church; it was placed beside the Bible on the altar at the Council of Trent.

It would be false to conclude that St. Thomas has never met with reverses or hostility. He was too advanced for some of his contemporaries, too conservative for others, and, in any case, provocative enough to invite criticism and opposition. He was between two distinct currents of opinion: the Augustinian School on the one hand, and the Aristotelian Averroists on the other. What neither side could see was that he was more Augustinian and at the same time more Aristotelian than either of them, since he derived his own doctrine from the confluence of these two streams.

There were, then as always, conservatives and progressivists, rationalists and mystics. There were also rival schools, each with its keen adherents, regulars and seculars, Franciscans and Dominicans. It was inevitable that St. Thomas, although almost universally venerated, should frighten some, even of his brethren, and offend others. All greatness knows these trials, and it is fortunate if they do not succeed in paralyzing talent and hindering progress.

Albert the Great, who was the first to encounter this opposition, defended himself with vigorous language. St. Thomas did otherwise; he simply went on fearlessly and without anger. It is something of a surprise to the historian, reading these peaceful and impartial pages, to find that they were written in painful circumstances, when the dispute was at its height. Absorbed in deep thinking, he was unmoved by strife, intellectual or practical; it simply made him concentrate more on his thoughts. We today, now that his enemies are no more, imagine that this attitude was easy to adopt, but at the time it must have been heroic. Thus, his reverses only add to his glory. Never was there a calmer navigator in a storm; he braved the deep, sure of his course and confident that his ship was seaworthy, and he suited his tactics to the varying conditions of the sea.

His followers did not show the same patience. They answered the pamphlet entitled "Corrections of Frater Thomas" by one called "Corrections of the Corruptors of Frater Thomas," but this little controversy was without great consequences. What was more important was the attitude of some authorities. The Bishop of Paris, Stephen Tempier, avoided condemning him when he presided over the famous dispute that led to the condemnation of thirteen doctrinal propositions. In 1277, three years after the death of the saint, he made up for it by condemning, among others, twenty Thomistic propositions. About the same time, an English Dominican named Robert Kilwardby, Archbishop of Canterbury, censured his doctrine, as did his successor, the Franciscan John Peckham. The dispute continued until his canonization on July 18, 1323, and it needed the direct intervention of the Holy

See, in 1324, to lift the ban that had been put on his writings forty-seven years before.

Yet these conflicts, doctrinal or personal, were merely incidental. St. Thomas's greatness was established, never again to be called in question. He foresaw this himself to some extent, as we can gather from some of his own statements. In spite of his humility, he speaks as one who dominates all time and addresses himself to the future, rather than to his own changing age. One might expect that he should feel a certain exhilaration, should himself be conscious of that glory which was to be showered upon him.

There is, however, one very important and quite authentic incident that shows us his true attitude. On December 6, 1273, while he was saying Mass in the Chapel of St. Nicholas at Naples, he had one of his customary ecstasies, but of longer duration. When he came out of it, he confided to Brother Reginald, "*Venit finis scripturae meae:* 'my writing has come to an end.' " And when his friend pressed him to finish his great work of the *Summa*, he replied, "Reginald, I can do no more. All that I have written seems now to me as so much straw."

Some chroniclers add that he ordered the *Summa* to be burned, but there is no historical evidence for this, and it is unlikely. What does seem certain is that, as the result of a vivid intuition, or possibly of a real vision, he lost all desire to write and that, in this supreme realization of his own inadequacy, he cried, "I can do no more."

It would not be very surprising if his continuous work over so many years, without any respite, should bring on some sort of mental fatigue, but there is certainly another consideration that might explain his resolve to cease writing.

Writing to Goethe of Beethoven's last years, Zelter says, "His works seemed to give him a secret horror." Zelter himself said, after composing his Ninth Symphony, and his Mass in *Re*, "I seem to have written but a few notes." There is a striking resemblance between these utterances and that of St. Thomas. The greater the genius, the more conscious he is of his own shortcomings. "Self-knowledge is the death of hope." When a man has easily achieved the difficult, he turns to the impossible. Especially in philosophy, every statement is a partial error, and silence is the whole truth. For us mortals, silence is the supreme expression of knowledge and comes only when one has experienced this pure intuition: *Près de qui tout savoir est un entassement.*[38]

Paul Valéry writes: "I am so doubtful about the connections of things, that I speak no more . . . I have not the courage to examine the details of this flash, which instantly throws a light on years of thought."

St. Thomas began with the question: *What is God?* Thence, by an unbroken, never-receding route, he reached his ecstasy in God, in which his human force spent itself. This was as it should be. "All higher life begins and ends with its gods." Our poor thoughts are as nothing in comparison with the Unknowable. In the end the prey must devour its pursuer.

The realization of the sublime unity of created things, as seen in God, must make a philosopher feel that his former account of them, by cause and effect, was a farce. As seen in God, and quite apart from the mystery of God himself, the created world is mystery enough, and to this also is due the final homage of silence.

St. Thomas tried to describe *things*, and succeeded in sketching only their outlines and silhouettes, exact and of great value, amid

[38] "In comparison with which, all knowledge is a mere heap" (Péguy).

so many perverted notions, but mere shadows for all that. He had lost faith in the possibility of grasping the ever-growing infinity of truth. He had learned "that perfect teaching, that perfect knowledge of his own nothingness, that abdication, which is in the heart of every truly great man." He had triumphed. He was enthusiastically hailed at his death as the "morning star," but he had seen a light greater than his own, and human knowledge lay behind him, never more to be pursued.

But he is not saddened: the change is too happy. God gives him the truth, which his mind of its own accord could not grasp, and his own powerlessness only emphasizes the infinite power of God. He felt himself consummated in God and had nothing for which to live, for true glory, as he says, is to be found only in God. He had no ambition to make his doctrine a permanent monument to his memory: he was to pale before the pure light of his teaching. He gradually withdrew within himself. His humility had saved him from falling as so many great minds have fallen, but he knew that in his self-abasement, he was drawing nearer to God.

The end drew near. He devoted his last efforts to a commentary on the Canticle of Canticles. He died before the Host, as Bayard before the cross of his sword-hilt, and he was delivered from the phantoms and futile abstractions of this world, to contemplate Truth itself. A being *thinks*, only because it is imperfect. In his ecstatic glimpses of God, St. Thomas attained the right henceforth to forget his thought.

This supreme abdication makes us, his disciples, only venerate him the more, love him more intensely, and join our humble homage and filial loyalty to the greater praise which is his in heaven.

Chapter Ten

St. Thomas's Influence Today

There are today two classes of people who take an interest in St. Thomas: the historians and the philosophers; those who treat him sympathetically as a giant of the past, and those who find him still an active force. Or, to borrow a metaphor from M. Thibaudet, there are those who regard his work as a beautiful waterfall, and those who wish to utilize its energy.

With both classes, it is evident that St. Thomas has come into his own. One general reason for this revival is that the twentieth century is doing for medieval philosophy what the nineteenth did for medieval art. Both are parts of the same great movement, and their comparison is instructive and might make us apprehensive. The revival in art brought about by Chateaubriand, Montalembert, Ozanam, Victor Hugo, Cartier, and Viollet-le-Duc was a sham. Then the error was acknowledged, and we drifted into Modernism. A parallel movement in philosophy, it will be argued, is leading to the attempts of the neo-Thomists, imitators of the thirteenth century, but with no more future than has the neo-Gothic in architecture. St. Thomas for them is merely an individual belonging to a forgotten century.

This, we submit, is where the comparison fails. Beauty is concerned primarily with external expression. If it were only a matter of the unchanging element in art, we could do today what was done at Chartres and in the Parthenon, in the days when men cared less about novelty, or when these works were in their infancy. Witness Rodin, Bourdelle, the brothers Perret and M. Le Corbusier. Now philosophy, too, has its substance and its external expression, and we are ready to make admissions about the latter, which some, perhaps, would not expect from us. But the substance is of the utmost importance, because here it is no longer principally a question of a state of mind, as in art, but of objective truth: not the free expression of one's own idea of reality but of reality itself.

Those who look upon philosophy as a sort of "work of art" might argue otherwise and maintain that the parallel holds completely. For them, the entire effort of thought in interpreting the universe gravitates toward experimental science: beyond that, there is only "poetic creation," which varies indefinitely with the varying imaginations of men and ages. We cannot here enter into controversy; we simply point out that this view is a denial of philosophy, because it arbitrarily deprives it of its proper object.

Philosophy is a study of the world based on the most exalted intellectual notions, which are abstracted from the things themselves; it is even more objective than experimental science. Therefore, it is not to be treated as a work of art. A successful genius in any branch of knowledge, and in any age, compels not only our admiration but our mental assent, which is the homage exacted by truth. We admire a work of art because it pleases us, or because its author is inspired. We assent to a philosophical thesis because it is true, and it makes no difference whether it comes from the thirteenth century or from the twentieth.

It is a bad omen when those who claim to represent their generation, and to be working for the progress of generations to come, disdain a great doctrine on the pretext that it is ancient. Those who really forge ahead are those who feel the support of the past behind them. "The teaching of the past," writes Nietzsche, "is the teaching of an oracle. You understand it only if you are a builder for the future, and a visionary of the present." The converse is equally true.

St. Thomas was a man of his times; he wished to serve his own generation, as all men should. This was not merely virtue but wisdom as well, even from the point of view of posterity. The thinker who claims to work for some abstract posterity will work feebly for all, like an artist trying to paint man in general.

Our Lord, whose mission was universal, was nonetheless a Jew, and a Jew of the time of Tiberias. A philosophy, even a universal philosophy, will not be fundamentally any the less a philosophical product of a certain epoch and of certain surroundings. And, just as our Lord's being a Jew did not hinder him from being Son of Man, so the fact that St. Thomas's philosophy was written between 1250 and 1274 does not prevent it from being fundamentally an eternal philosophy — the *philosophia quaedam perennis* that Leibnitz sought after.

In writing for his own age, St. Thomas has written for all ages, because he went below the foundations of his own age and found the eternal principles of things. Truth is "older than the idea which we have of it," as Pascal says, and surely it is more lasting than we are, especially when, as in metaphysics, it is concerned with objects outside time.

In fact, Thomistic philosophy in its youth and today are not contradictory. Those principles at which we marvel were once new; they seem rather arid now, because they have lost their bloom.

The truth contained in ideas derives its cogency from reality itself, and reality from God himself, so that, indirectly, truth is from God, and therefore defies the ravages of time. That which is lasting in the realms of reality is lasting also in true thought, and the true thought of the future will find it again. Hence, to disdain any truth is to offend against that eternal activity ever at work in the world of things, and in the human mind.

We need to take up again this ancient wisdom, which is at once the most humbling and most ennobling of creeds. Never has man so scorned human authority as he does today, when he has rejected that of God. He repudiates tradition and all teaching, and is a slave to every fleeting attraction, because he will not be the free servant of truth.

Indocility of this kind was foreign to St. Thomas's character. He made use of the past, as something eternally present, which furnished him with the elements of a new teaching. His great interest to us is due to this fact that he satisfied the needs of his own age by borrowing from antiquity. With equal loyalty, should not we be free to do the same?

At certain epochs, and particularly, I suppose, in the days of Descartes, Thomists sincerely believed that they had the right and duty to modify the Thomist system in its very foundations, in order to bring it into line with newly found needs. We may praise their broad-mindedness, but, insofar as they changed its object, they gave way to weakness, by allowing themselves to be overpowered by the intellectual activity of their age, when their principles were quite sound and merely needed adapting.

Thomism suffered in those days because its adherents, while holding its externals, never bothered to consult its author, or to be guided by his principles. The scholastic method, which never restricted St. Thomas, because he used it as a method, and not as a strait-waistcoat, began to paralyze the brains of his followers. They deferred to his authority without mastering his thought, and there can be no living philosophy without such mastery.

Hence, the modern revival of Thomism must be a renovation, and an effort to go deeper into St. Thomas's meaning. The revival may not as yet be firmly established, but it is still being attempted, and that is a sign that the philosophy bears the mark of continuity that we claim for it. Give a thing to time, says Carlyle, and, if it prospers, it is a good thing. This is even a truer test when a thing revives, after being spoiled by its misguided guardians.

The chief objection that is brought, sincerely or otherwise, against the possibility of a revival in Thomistic philosophy is that this philosophy is based on a now discredited idea of the world, and on cosmology, physics, and even psychology, which science will no longer endorse. It is geocentric and anthropocentric, which is quite opposed to our modern conception of our position in the universe. It is solidly realist, whereas the prevailing philosophical current is idealist and nominalist.

The same objection is brought against Christianity itself, the dogmas of which are said to depend upon the same narrow conception of the universe. In both cases, the error is due to lack of knowledge. Sometimes with the best will in the world, and often with great feeling, these objectors falsify everything, because they merely skim the surface. As Albert the Great would have said, "They blaspheme what they do not know."

A noted French physicist, in a preface that does him no honor, speaks of Christianity and of science in terms that are simply silly. It would make him blush to tax him with them in serious company. Less trivial and obviously sincere is M. Pierre Lasserre, who comes to the same conclusion in his *Ernest Renan*. But his presentation of Thomism is invariably incorrect. How, then, it may be asked, can his conclusions be of value or his criticism well founded? Criticism is our strong point nowadays; indeed, it is our only one. It has great value, but not when its basis is wrong, and in the present case, it obviously is so.

It is not true that Thomism, much less Christianity, depends on a defunct theory of physics or cosmology. We have proved this of Christianity elsewhere,[39] by a simple exposition of its doctrines in the light of current thought. As for Thomism, it is beyond the scope of this book to discuss the problem in all its details, but the following summary should prove sufficient.

Thomism, as a philosophy, is essentially metaphysical. Cosmology and physics, not to mention working hypotheses in psychology (which are classifications rather than parts of a system), are not part of its essential makeup. It is obvious that the geocentric theory will greatly affect the way a thirteenth-century writer expresses his doctrine, but it is elementary criticism to distinguish between the fundamental ideas of a metaphysician and the means whereby he expresses them — those accessory facts which inevitably present themselves to a thinker, because of the ideas common to an age, which color the thought of the individual.

Metaphysical doctrines go through two phases. At first, they are in the mind, in a pure state, but lacking all coordination with experience, and therefore incommunicable. The second phase is a

[39] *Catéchisme des Incroyants*.

sort of individuation, when the idea is mingled with a heap of notions derived from experience, and true, more or less, according to the state of experimental knowledge. This may somewhat tarnish the original idea, but it does not destroy its truth in its own order.

I might express the notion of providence by saying that God directs atoms as well as souls. Now, the fact that the atomic theory is no longer held does not invalidate my notion of providence. And if I use the theory of atoms in my proof of providence, as St. Thomas uses the sun, "the source of all heat," my proof will not be rendered invalid because the theory of atoms has given way to a theory of force. Such a conclusion would show ignorance of the very nature of a metaphysical problem and of the method of solving it.

M. Pierre Lasserre imagines, as others have done, that "the ideal world of Plato or of St. Thomas is only an idealization of the world as it appeared to them, with their scanty scientific data." Nothing could be further from the truth. The ideal world of St. Thomas (we may leave out Plato, whose true position is still uncertain) is an agglomeration of the necessary data of all experience, even the most elementary and, therefore, most stable. It does not depend, therefore, on the progress of experimental knowledge, but simply on the progress of the mind.

When we are given as an example the theory that man is the principal end of creation, we must not treat it as a metaphysical theory, but as a *belief* founded on limited experience. What *is* metaphysical, and therefore as valid now as then, is that matter is ordained to form, body to soul, as the less to the greater, and the partial to the total, which is its ultimate end.

We admit that, in the Middle Ages, knowledge was represented as a unity; hence its beauty. In every progressive age, the attempt at unification begins anew. But the unity reached is always provisional, like the unity of a body and its daily nourishment; it is not of its essence. It is much more a link for connecting minds, and methods of exposition; it is not properly a unity of doctrine.

Further, it is certainly not to this kind of unity that we refer when we praise the synthesis of St. Thomas. A complete synthesis, comprising all experimental science, will always be, absolutely speaking, an impossibility. A relatively complete synthesis will require restating every twenty years. But a metaphysical synthesis is quite another thing, and on a different plane. It is not unrelated to the other, and therefore there is, and always will be, the possibility of restating the ancient doctrine. But the doctrine will be just the same, with merely a new presentation and a new line of development.

We may add that, while St. Thomas certainly made use of the science of his day, he often shows his aloofness from and even mistrust of theories, which he realized were only a temporary vogue. Even when he makes no such proviso, his cautious language, his general principles, his concern with first causes and unconcern with contingencies make it equally clear.

Secondly, it would be wrong to imagine that this physics and cosmology, so oddly out-of-date as a whole, is therefore worthless. The great writers of antiquity have not labored in vain. In their errors about facts, and in their maladjustment of true data, there are flashes of true genius, intuitions that modern science has confirmed from a different standpoint and expressed in different, although closely allied, form.

In particular, St. Thomas's metaphysics of God is believed by some to depend on out-of-date ideas. This is easily disproved. After what we have said of metaphysics in general, the following should be a sufficient defense. To St. Thomas, the universe, created by God, is absolutely and wholly contingent, in its form, duration, and being. He held the possibility of an eternal, solitary God or, on the other hand, of an eternal world. He held likewise that the world could have been created quite different from what it is, with entirely different laws. Now, he could not have maintained that the world was contingent in this way, especially in its form, if he had begun by deriving his God from the creature.

Voltaire's ironic epigram, "It is said that God created man to his own image: man has retaliated," is applicable to Deism, or to the various emanationist forms of Pantheism, but not to St. Thomas's conception of God. He places the divine essence far above forms subject to time, and even grants that "God has no essence."[40]

Again, the problem of the relations of faith and reason is treated in the Thomistic synthesis, principally as a metaphysical problem, as its very nature necessitates. In the realm of contingency, then as now, our data can be accepted as data, on the supposition that it is revealed.

To sum up, the essential part of the Thomistic synthesis does not belong exclusively to any particular era, and may therefore just as well belong to our own. Once granted that metaphysics is an autonomous science, and granted the principle of faith, we may hold it without fear of being behind the times. It does not deal with something time-bound, but with something that rises free of time and dominates the whole course of time.

This does not mean that we must adopt St. Thomas's didactic method. After all, it was not his creation, but the custom of his

[40] *De Ente et Essentia*, ch. 6.

times. He perfected it in many ways, but only relatively to his times. Again the problems that he proposed and his particular point of view were governed by the stage of knowledge at the time, by his audience, and by his controversies. These are only a covering or shell; they are not the fruit.

The fruit itself would be of the utmost value in these days, when, despite our pretensions, we are so impoverished. These are times of topsy-turvydom, with all the wealth of materials: '*Un rien infiniement riche*," as Paul Valéry says. Chateaubriand, even in his day, denounced "the invasion of ideas, following upon the barbarian invasion." A modern German philosopher describes current thought as a "pathological interregnum." Nietzsche calls it "a joyless, *forceless* critique."

We could easily multiply such examples, but it is not necessary in order to bring home the fact that our philosophers, when we ask for bread, give us a stone. Their brilliant theories may open up certain avenues of thought; on the other hand, they many simply obscure the issue, and the net result is neither illuminating nor reassuring. Chaos rules thought and leads to a kind of triumphant failure. We find an eager curiosity about philosophical systems, together with disdain of the truth, or utter despair of ever attaining it.

It is not that we lack the men. We have plenty of theories, detailed analyses, penetration, and breadth of outlook. But we have no order, no general rules of the intelligence drawn from first principles or from the First Principle. We are "ever learning and never attaining to the knowledge of the truth."[41] These men speak

[41] 2 Tim. 3:7.

wisely on occasion, but at other times, they leave the impression that to become a philosopher is to lose your reason. And judging by their supineness in making up their minds, they do not know themselves when they have spoken wisely.

In short, we are weary of thinkers and want a little truth. The crisis through which society is passing, and which makes every thinking man apprehensive, is fundamentally a crisis of doctrine. If the eye be faulty, what chance have the limbs to act well? There is a worldwide cry for peace; peace implies order, and order comes primarily from thought. And we have no thought wise enough and comprehensive enough to assist us.

The remedy is to be found in religion. We must renew our youth by a pact with God, as Faust renewed his by a pact with the Devil. But religion will help us only if it assumes an intellectual character. We must have a philosophy, and what better one than that which the Church has declared to be most suited to her teaching and tendencies? Thomism is not an archeological specimen, but a living force, capable of supplying the help we need.

St. Thomas was a master of order, a guide of minds, a wise man. In the midst of ever-shifting uncertainty, he found a firm foothold: his vantage-point was high enough to enable him to help a much wider public than that for which he wrote. To all our differences and serious disputes he applies the salve of truth; he lends to our resources the power of his broad and ever-adaptable synthesis. He is uncompromising only with regard to this framework and these general principles, without which the mind is unbalanced, and reality untruly centered.

Therefore, in advocating Thomism, we are not advocating a return to the thirteenth century. We are urging men to follow the right path, not to retrace their steps. We have wandered far from the right path, and a return to it is not a retrograde step.

Nowadays, every system starts *ab ovo*.[42] We, however, are not urging a *repetition* of St. Thomas's philosophy, and, if there are, here and there, signs of such a tendency, no sensible person, nobody with any breadth of mind, should be misled by them. Every religion has its true worshipers and its fanatics. There is a kind of worship that makes us want to blaspheme, but it would be silly to do so, for we would thereby fall into the very excess that we deplore. No, the true way to be a Thomist is to seek truth, wisdom, enlightened religion to an extent ever more ambitious and never satisfied. That is to be a Thomist of the school of St. Thomas himself, and not of the dabblers in Thomism.

The notion has long since been dead and buried that to be a Thomist means to belong to a past age and to be out of touch with one's own. Every lover of philosophy can find in Thomism something to think about, some weapon, some instruction. And he may even find that it solves the difficulties that lie at the very roots of knowledge.

[42] From the beginning; literally, "from the egg."

Chapter Eleven

The Future of St. Thomas

We have already said that there are two classes of people today interested in St. Thomas: those whose interest is in the past, and those whose interest is in the present. We must now subdivide the latter class. There are the dilettanti who take it up today and drop it tomorrow. There are also the disillusioned, the desperate, who will make for any port in a storm. Not quite sure whether Thomism is true, they find in it a certain note of hope, and that is all they want; it is all that many people want in their religion.

All we need say of the dilettanti is that their Thomism is rather puerile, and that they merely stand in the way of the true revival. We cannot imagine that it has any future when we compare this flimsy, halfhearted support with the severity of its object.

We may show more sympathy toward the despairing, but they are equally disquieting. Philosophy and despair have nothing in common, since the latter lacks all guarantee of stability.

The real Thomist, then, will welcome only those who believe that there is an opening for Thomism, who are willing to help, and consequently prepared to submit to the conditions that we have still to enumerate.

It might be thought that a doctrine recognized as sound would compel universal assent by its own intrinsic merits, without being worked up into a doctrine that could no longer be called Thomism.

This objection I have often met with: it was put when I attempted to sketch in up-to-date language some of St. Thomas's foundational writings. Some would prefer that the doctrine was left in its original austere garb, where nobody could use it while others, with the best intentions, never face the facts.

It is impossible that Thomism should have a future — outside specialist circles — if left in its original medieval dress. If we merely put it forward without readapting and renewing it, it will certainly not have a lasting revival. A few willing oars may take it a few lengths, but ere long it will be swept out to sea. Our ideas have advanced, not in worth, but in the way in which they are expressed and discussed. We must be abreast of the times in this respect, even though our doctrine be identical with St. Thomas's. It is as true of a system as it is of a man that he "becomes a novice at every stage of his life."

If scholastics have been at fault, it is in thinking that Thomism could just go on indefinitely without a crisis — that is, without a fundamental readjustment, of the kind that nature effects in certain organs at the age of puberty, or after a serious breakdown. New conditions and new problems have, in the past, called for a change of point of view, which has never been effected. It was called for by Galileo, by Descartes, by Kant, and it looks as though it were surely called for now by Bergson.

St. Thomas is thoroughly medieval; his images and sense experience belong to his times. It is only his doctrine that can belong to our time, because it is outside all time. The defense of this latter proposition implies an acceptance of the former, since it is based on the distinction between what is alive and what is dead in a philosophy.

It is not enough to re-edit Thomism and defend it vigorously: we must rejuvenate it. It is only a fresh, living thing that can begin a new movement.

Since St. Thomas's time, we have made progress, even if not always in the right direction. The *Summa* is not the sum-total of knowledge, nor a complete repository of eternal truth. Or rather, we may say that it is a complete synthesis, containing all knowledge virtually, and this knowledge can always be made more and more explicit.

St. Thomas's writings do not even contain the whole of Thomism, any more than the Gospels contain the whole of Catholicism, or the grain of mustard-seed the whole kingdom of heaven. The Scriptures are a witness to religion, not the whole of it; they contain it in germ, not in its developed state. In the same way, Thomism is the development of an original germ; the germ is the principles and metaphysical theses. To be disloyal to these is to be no longer a Thomist. On the other hand, to strive to preserve the problems and solutions in their original form, in their original presentation, and their original relations to experience is to make it a barren doctrine, a sacred mummy, and not a living force.

This applies to any great doctrine. Its solutions, even when true, are always provisional. Time, which corrodes everything, soon plays havoc with many of them, and the synthesis has to be renovated. Metaphysics can never be adequately and finally expressed in temporal, ever-changing language, since it is outside time. Even the most lasting formulas are only so many stages at which we stop for a time, before going forward. To look upon them as the terminus would be a betrayal of our intelligence. There can be no end, properly speaking, to the pursuit of philosophy.

This does not imply that philosophy has no firm foundations. We cannot insist too strongly on the correlative truths: eternity of the essential, mortality of its incarnations; necessary assent to the ever-prevailing essence, necessary renewal of the successive forms and adaptations.

The true critic is he who takes into consideration this twofold necessity, who shows that he understands St. Thomas by rewriting him freely and by bringing him into touch with modern thought, by a genuine metamorphosis. A genuine metamorphosis is one that acts according to nature, like the production of a butterfly from a chrysalis.

Thomism, moreover, is not only a doctrine but also a method, or better, an attitude. We have portrayed St. Thomas at work. When he met with some new point of view, or with contradiction, or an adverse doctrine, he did not buttress up his own view. No, he examined his findings with discrimination, and seems more eager to assimilate than to combat them. Once he had modified and corrected them, he was prepared to use them for his own growth. His whole life shows this tendency; it is a consequence of his independence and breadth of mind. And surely we should be like him in this respect.

St. Thomas never meant his system to be exclusive or watertight. He wrote for all who think, in order to exchange ideas and to harmonize his thoughts with theirs. He expected his followers to do likewise and would have been horrified at their clinging to his apron-strings and refusing to move with the times.

Much still remained unsaid. Nothing that he said could express adequately the fullness and unfathomable depths of truth, but he at least had due respect for what he could not adequately explain. He counted on the collaboration of others for the development of various problems. The future might be able to find out what in his days was unknown.

Now what, in the light of modern science, are the gaps and shortcomings in St. Thomas's work? It is not easy to say, and it will always be subject to differences of opinion, but I think that most people will agree on the following.

St. Thomas's exposition is tinged with a kind of formalism due to his associations with Aristotle, and to the method prevalent in his day. Not that he has lost sight of reality, as so many did, for whom science became a mere logic-chopping and juggling with abstract terms. His sound judgment saved him from this. But even while his conclusions remain true, the concrete elements of the problem are not always put forward in an intellectual way. He is rather in the air, and his writings, for all their substantial richness, are presented in a way that seems rather stinted and sparse, and, for us who are realists and word-conscious, not very adaptable.

St. Thomas himself taught that it is the individual that is real, not the logical framework; that science must be in touch with the concrete, which is the end of knowledge.[43] One does not easily evade a whole century's persistent pressure. We know the stir that the discovery of Aristotle's *Organon* caused in the Middle Ages. There is no question but that St. Thomas, were he alive today, would write in quite a different strain and marshal his proofs in quite a different manner.

It may be simply a question of style, but, after all, style is fundamental to the communication of thought. All medieval writers and their commentators have a tendency to fill up the gaps in their experience with *a priori* notions, and to substitute conventional symbolism for scientific observation. These may satisfy the dialectician, but they hardly take us very far into reality.

[43] Cf. *Summa Theologica*, I, Q. 34, art. 8.

Nature is visualized in the schools as a series of cog-wheels, agents and recipients, causes and effects, whose interplay is determined by unchangeable essences and fixed qualities derived therefrom. This takes the place of the changing complexus, growing ever more unified as we probe it more deeply, which science reveals. It follows that, in a number of theses, even in the proofs of the existence of God, the physicist is at a loss to find where to classify his discoveries under the logical labels used in the text. Well-meaning thinkers have said as much to me, and I must, to some extent, admit it. The harsh and, to my mind, unjust strictures of M. Le Roy, on the Thomistic proofs of the existence of God, while traceable in part to his personal views, are also due to this abstract formalism, which looks so like a mere matter of words, and must, for the needs of today, be made more positive. Nothing could be easier to do, in principle at least, since it only implies a change of externals. But it has not been done and must be included in the agenda of modern Thomism.

Again, it often treats of man's various faculties and psychological characteristics, not as terms in analysis, but as distinct entities, thereby destroying the unity of life, and sometimes rendering their interrelations almost unintelligible. St. Thomas avoided this fault; he was far better informed than most of his disciples, even his modern disciples, and his genius intervened to save the situation, when it might have proved extremely dangerous for doctrine. Still, there is that impression: the method tends to confuse us and greatly to lessen the value of the conclusions.

Quite generally speaking, it must be admitted that the part played by abstract logic in the works of St. Thomas, as in those of Aristotle, is disproportionate. His method of exegesis is a striking instance in point and may serve as typical. If we take the Psalter, a work obviously compiled without any motive of theology or mysticism, we find that St. Thomas, by ingenious analysis, has discovered in it a whole ideological order, rather like the battles that Leonardo da Vinci imagined he saw in the crevices of ancient ramparts. However fallacious this procedure may be, it is quite innocuous; but once it is introduced into philosophy, only a genius of more than ordinary judgment can prevent it from having dire consequences.

The Thomism of today must give up these excesses of a method which is valuable in itself, but, because of these excesses, brings the doctrine that it expounds into bad repute. We want less abstract reasoning and more facts, and more control by facts; more abundant use of positive science, even in Metaphysics, and *a fortiori* in psychology and ethics, and above all in social ethics. St. Thomas's anatomy of reality is wonderful: it is even too plentiful, for, as Michelangelo "invented muscles," St. Thomas invents, or reinvents faculties such as the *senses communis*, *appetitus concupiscibilis*, and *iracibilis*. But the biology of reality, so to call it: the study of the environment, internal and external, of these elements has still to be developed, if we wish his admirable philosophy to be something more than a museum piece, and to become a living doctrine for all.

My fellow Thomists might be tempted to deem this criticism lacking in respect. I reply in the words of Péguy: "A great philosophy is not one that has no breaches in its walls, but one which has fortresses." We must beware, lest a false respect on the part of its adherents should lead to a loss of respect and to abandonment on the part of those outside. We wish to spread St. Thomas's philosophy as a living force in the future, not as a literary monument. Therefore, it must steep itself in modern life; it must follow the progress of science and modern philosophy, as far as these are sober, in order to bring about what must come someday — namely, a new *Summa*, summarizing contemporary thought, as St. Thomas's *Summa* summarized the thought of the past.

For it is our ideal that the Thomism of the future should be characterized epoch from epoch, by successive syntheses, while retaining unchanged the continuity of its line of thought. Such a doctrine cannot perish, but it must be renewed periodically. Those who would "preserve" it are merely preparing for its fall. Only what is eternal survives; temporal things grow or die, or rather grow by partially dying in order to be born again, only what is immortal in them remaining unchanged.

The circumstances that gave rise to Thomism are dead, its problems are dead, its method and vocabulary are dead; but the doctrine is not affected by clearing out this debris. The mollusk sheds its outer shell and makes a new one; the shell is not essential to it. A great doctrine is not identical with any of its ephemeral creations; it depends on something much deeper.

Anyone not accustomed to deep thinking, who merely burdens his memory with a lot of ready-made formula, is lost as soon as the expressions are changed. Again, those who know a system only by its exterior forms, like the silhouette of a tree, are shocked or grieved if anyone strips the bark off their tree, and lops off its branches to make it grow better. But anyone who really understands the life of the tree will recognize it just as easily by its stunted branches, and by its sap, as by its full branches and foliage.

Fundamentally, Thomism, like any other philosophy, does not depend upon its ideological symbols, taken in a material sense, but rather, on the profound relations that they are used to represent. Matter and form, substance and accident are terms that might be discarded without modifying either the life or the results of Thomism. Not that I propose their abolition; all I mean is that the principle is not fantastic in the light of modern thought.

We need a Thomism that will be to St. Thomas's work what the New Testament is to the Old — without, of course, the intervention of a divine Person.

Thomism will always be one of the great treasures of humanity, and St. Thomas will be its leader and its greatest example. His insight into things visible and invisible, and his incarnation of wisdom in things are a wonderful heritage. If, in the near future, it were adopted, it would greatly help in the restoration and harmony of thought, and the promotion of peace and order in practical affairs, and we should be able to await, but with more confidence, the realization of M. Gonzague de Reynold's vision of hope: "We are living in a nebula, but a nebula which may become a star. If it should do so for an élite, it will be the first sign of reconstruction, the first hope of a new world."

Biographical Note

Antonin Gilbert Sertillanges
(1863-1948)

Born in the French city of Clermont-Ferrand on November 16, 1863, A. G. Sertillanges entered the Dominican Order twenty years later, taking the religious name Dalmatius. In 1888, he was ordained a priest.

After completing his studies and teaching for a few years, Fr. Sertillanges was appointed secretary of the prestigious scholarly journal *Revue Thomiste*. In 1900, he became professor of moral theology at the Catholic Institute in Paris, where he taught for twenty years. Later, Fr. Sertillanges taught elsewhere in France and also in Holland. During his year-long stay in Jerusalem in 1923, he was inspired to write *What Jesus Saw from the Cross*.

His classic book *The Intellectual Life* explains the methods, conditions, habits, and virtues that are necessary in the intellectual life. These virtues bore great fruit in Fr. Sertillanges' own life, enabling him to become a widely recognized expert in the philosophy of St. Thomas Aquinas and to write many books and more than a thousand articles in the areas of philosophy, theology, art, and spirituality.

But Fr. Sertillanges was far more than a professor and scholar. During his lifetime, he was widely admired for his skill as a preacher, a spiritual director, and an apologist, and was particularly successful in presenting the Faith in compelling terms to the young and to the unconverted.

No "ivory tower" intellectual, but first and foremost a passionate son of the Church, Fr. Sertillanges wrote numerous works that bridge the gap that often yawns today between academic theology and the everyday faith of the ordinary layman.

The fruit of both hard study and devout prayer, and motivated by the desire to preach Catholic truth *usque ad mortem* ("unto death," in the words of the Dominican motto), the works of Fr. Sertillanges are now informing and inspiring yet another generation of readers in these times of theological uncertainty and moral disarray.

Sophia Institute

Sophia Institute is a nonprofit institution that seeks to nurture the spiritual, moral, and cultural life of souls and to spread the Gospel of Christ in conformity with the authentic teachings of the Roman Catholic Church.

Sophia Institute Press fulfills this mission by offering translations, reprints, and new publications that afford readers a rich source of the enduring wisdom of mankind.

Sophia Institute also operates two popular online Catholic resources: CrisisMagazine.com and CatholicExchange.com.

Crisis Magazine provides insightful cultural analysis that arms readers with the arguments necessary for navigating the ideological and theological minefields of the day. *Catholic Exchange* provides world news from a Catholic perspective as well as daily devotionals and articles that will help you to grow in holiness and live a life consistent with the teachings of the Church.

In 2013, Sophia Institute launched Sophia Institute for Teachers to renew and rebuild Catholic culture through service to Catholic education. With the goal of nurturing the spiritual, moral, and cultural life of souls, and an abiding respect for the role and work of teachers, we strive to provide materials and programs that are at once enlightening to the mind and ennobling to the heart; faithful and complete, as well as useful and practical.

Sophia Institute gratefully recognizes the Solidarity Association for preserving and encouraging the growth of our apostolate over the course of many years. Without their generous and timely support, this book would not be in your hands.

www.SophiaInstitute.com
www.CatholicExchange.com
www.CrisisMagazine.com
www.SophiaInstituteforTeachers.org